The Cambridge Manuals of Science and
Literature

T0352044

A HISTORY OF CIVILIZATION
IN PALESTINE

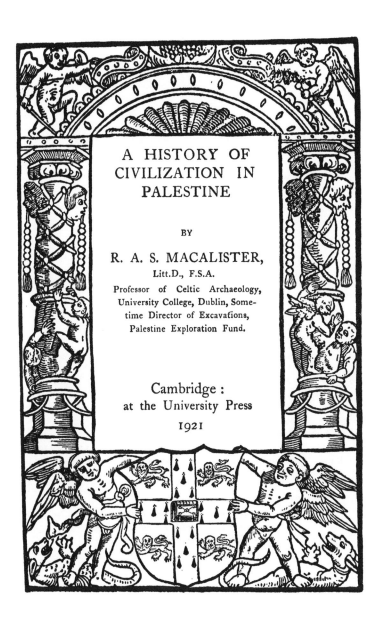

A HISTORY OF CIVILIZATION IN PALESTINE

BY

R. A. S. MACALISTER,

Litt.D., F.S.A.

Professor of Celtic Archaeology,
University College, Dublin, Some-
time Director of Excavations,
Palestine Exploration Fund.

Cambridge :
at the University Press

1921

CAMBRIDGE UNIVERSITY PRESS
Cambridge, New York, Melbourne, Madrid, Cape Town,
Singapore, São Paulo, Delhi, Tokyo, Mexico City

Cambridge University Press
The Edinburgh Building, Cambridge CB2 8RU, UK

Published in the United States of America by
Cambridge University Press, New York

www.cambridge.org
Information on this title: www.cambridge.org/9781107401655

© Cambridge University Press 1912

First published 1912
Reprinted 1921
First paperback edition 2011

A catalogue record for this publication is available from the British Library

ISBN 978-1-107-40165-5 Paperback

*With the exception of the coat of arms
at the foot, the design on the title page is a
reproduction of one used by the earliest known
Cambridge printer, John Siberch, 1521*

PREFACE

JUST forty years ago, as we write, Captain Warren made the first experiments in excavating in Palestine. Just twenty years ago Professor Petrie closed the work with which he inaugurated the era of scientific research. When Captain Warren began his work, it was expected by many that a few strokes of the spade would settle the questionings on Biblical subjects that were then being asked with ever increasing persistence. The dreams of the subscribers centred round records of David's wars and of Solomon's glory; the Ark of the Covenant and the idols of Manasseh; some, perhaps, hoped for a letter or two written by one privileged to hear the words of Him who spake as never man spake. Nothing of the kind has come to light, however, with the single exception of the Moabite Stone—and that was not discovered by a professed explorer, but lighted upon by accident by a travelling missionary who had no idea of the value of his 'find'!

On the other hand, we now look back through vistas of history unimagined forty years ago, and our way is illumined by strange lights breaking through from unexpected quarters. Here and there, no doubt, there are still dark corners which we may hope will some day be made clearer. We have obtained, not a bare confirmation, but what is far better, a wider comprehension of the familiar history.

It is a disastrous mistake to suppose that the aim of excavation is the discovery of contemporary written documents. They are most important, but it is very easy to exaggerate their value, especially when we are dealing with the ancient East. The monument of a vainglorious oriental king is not less fulsome, and not more convincing, than is a modern patent-medicine advertisement. The authority of a letter depends ultimately on the personality of its unknown writer. When (as has notoriously been the case in explorations in Assyria and Babylonia) tablets and bas-reliefs are made the chief purpose of the work, the humbler utensils that speak of the life and civilization of the country are apt to be neglected, and their essential value lost for ever by the destructive processes of the excavation itself.

It is also an error to suppose that the special function of an excavator is to *confirm* written history, sacred or profane. If this were so he would be the most useless of men. He calls the dead of the past from their graves, and, so far as he can, makes them live once more their lives before the spectators : but this imaginary *anastasis* cannot persuade those who hear not Moses and the Prophets any more effectively than would an actual resurrection. His duty is not to pencil over outlines already drawn, making no

impression on the sketch : his function is to fill
in the background, and to add the touches that
ultimately make a perfect picture. It is from this
point of view that the results of recent exploration
are regarded in the following pages.

In this, the second impression, some errors have
been corrected, and some modifications introduced,
necessitated by the momentous events which have
taken place since the book was first issued.

R. A. S. M.

CONTENTS

CHAP.   PAGE
       Preface   v
  I.   Palestine and its Earliest Inhabitants .   .   .   1
 II.   The Later Stone Age in Palestine   .   .   .   12
III.   The pre-Israelite Semitic Occupations .   .   .   26
 IV.   The First Struggle of West and East .   .   .   48
  V.   The Hebrew Monarchy   63
 VI.   The Captivities and After   70
VII.   The Growth of the Religious Consciousness in
       Israel   78
VIII. Roman and Byzantine   95
 IX.   Muslim and Crusader   107
  X.   Till Yesterday   117
       Bibliography   130
       Index   134

LIST OF ILLUSTRATIONS

FIG.   **PAGE**

1. Graffiti in a cave found at Gezer. (*From a drawing prepared for the Palestine Exploration Fund by the author and reproduced by permission of the Fund*) 14

2. One of the Kabûr Beni Isra'in. (*From a photograph by the author*) 19

3. A corner of a Palestinian Village. (*From a photograph by the author*) 35

4. A Philistine Captive. (*From a photograph by H. R. Hall, M.A., F.S.A., illustrating his article on the 'Discoveries in Crete' in the Proceedings of the Society of Biblical Archaeology, June 1909; reproduced by permission of the Society and of Mr Hall*) 51

5 & 6. Terra-cotta Plaques 'pourtraying the Queen of Heaven.' (*By permission of the Palestine Exploration Fund*) . . . . 90 & 91

7. Ruin of a Byzantine Village. (*From a photograph by Rev. Prof. G. A. Barton, Bryn Mawr*) . . . 99

8. Façade of the Ruined Synagogue at Meiron. (*From a photograph by the author*) 103

9. The Tombs of Kings Godfrey and Baldwin I. (*From Beauveau's 'Relation journalière du voyage du Levant'*) 114

Map of Palestine . . . . *at end*

CHAPTER I

A TRAVELLER landing at Jaffa and setting his face to the East, will in his journey pass through strangely varied scenes. The comparatively uninteresting and half-Europeanised town, from which he starts, lies surrounded by its famous orange groves, shadowed by waving palms and by sub-tropical trees and plants. These he leaves behind almost immediately. At first he traverses the plain of Sharon, a tract of magnificent fertility, yielding rich returns even to a people who have not progressed in scientific agriculture since the days of their Canaanite forefathers. After some ten or fifteen miles the scenery suddenly changes, and the traveller finds himself among rocky mountains, intersected by complex winding valleys. Many of these valleys have almost as rich possibilities as the plain, but the cultivated areas are now comparatively small. Traces of old terraces on the hill side shew that in former days there was much more extensive agricultural work

carried on here than at present. Rising among the
bare and rugged hills, the traveller at last reaches
the summit of the long chain, on the top of which
stand Jerusalem and Hebron, and which stretches
from Beersheba northward to lose itself in the maze
of the mountains of Ephraim. Crossing this, he finds
the opposite side to be yet more desolate than that
over which he has come—a waterless waste, full of
hills of an outline so unearthly as to suggest the
weird appearance of lunar scenery. At the bottom
of the eastern slope of the chain he finds himself in
the fertile but unhealthy depths of the Jordan valley.
Beyond the Jordan is the steep precipitous wall that
guards the pleasant uplands of Moab. Crossing these,
the traveller reaches at last the great highway which
year by year is trodden by the pilgrims from Damascus
to Mecca. And beyond is the trackless desert.

The river Jordan, flowing from north to south, is
a natural boundary between the western and the
eastern parts of the journey we have imagined : and
some words of description of this extraordinary river
are a necessary introduction to the study of the
country's physical features, with which this chapter
is principally concerned. It rises in the spurs of
Mount Hermon, about 1700 feet above sea-level.
Several powerful springs unite to form a single
stream, which, running down a marshy bed, expands,
after about 40 miles from the most northerly source,

into a picturesque little sheet of water now known as *Bahîret el-Hûleh* or 'Lakelet of Huleh.' The ancient name is lost[1]. At this point the surface is only six feet above sea-level, so that already there has been a considerable fall. Leaving Huleh it descends in a boiling torrent—dropping 687 feet in little over ten miles—and again expands, to form the lake called by the Hebrews the Sea of Chinnereth (from an unidentified region somewhere in its borders[2]) and in the New Testament known by the more familiar name of the Sea of Galilee, of Tiberias or of Gennesaret. From this it descends further, in a course so winding that though the distance in a straight line is only 60 miles, the actual length of the river is over 185. In this section it suffers a further fall of 610 feet, so that when at last it comes to an end in the bitter waters of the Dead Sea, it has reached a depth of nearly 1300 feet below the earth's surface. At the

---

[1] The current identification with the 'Waters of Merom' of Josh. xi. 5, 7, is without substantial foundation. This name does not necessarily denote a lake; more probably they were some group of mountain springs.

[2] It is popularly supposed that this name is derived from the Hebrew *kinnôr*, 'a harp,' on account of its harp-like shape. For several reasons the idea is inadmissible. The *map* of the sea looks not unlike a *modern* harp, but no one viewing the sea itself from any of the surrounding hill-tops would be struck by any such resemblance: and a name such as this is of course far older than any map. For a reference to the region of this name see 1 Kings xv. 20.

deepest part of the sea itself the soundings give an additional 1300 feet : the bottom of the valley is therefore, at its lowest point, sunk some 2600 feet below sea-level.

Could we transport ourselves back to the Pleistocene period; to the remote beginning of the Quaternary, the last of the ages of the world's geological history ; we should experience very different geographical conditions. Instead of the ever-deepening valley with its rushing river and its three lakes, we should find a huge inland sea, filled by the drainage of the Lebanon glaciers and snows. Of this lake the Dead Sea is the shrunken representative.

The *maritime plain* extends by the shore of the tideless Mediterranean, along the entire length of the country : its breadth, however, varies greatly at different points. At the south end it is some 35 miles across, or even more. As we proceed upwards it narrows gradually, being bounded on the one side by a coast-line that trends eastward, on the other by a line of mountains running almost due north and south. At the latitude of Jaffa the breadth is about 15 miles. The mountains from this point northwards gradually approximate to the coast, till at last the spur of Carmel shoots into the sea, reducing the coast plain to the width of the causeway round the foot of the promontory. Passing Carmel, we find ourselves at the entrance to the great plain, known in old days as

the Plain of Jezreel or of Esdraelon, and now called
the Merj Ibn 'Amr—'The Plain of 'Amr's Son.' This
plain drives like a wedge through the mountain
system, and has always been the chief highway to the
interior of the country—though in winter, after heavy
rain, it becomes a dangerous slough, the soft earth being
turned to mud quite deep enough in places to make
the transit one of considerable risk. It is proverbially
the battlefield of Palestine: so much so that it is
adopted by the seer of visions on Patmos as the type
of the final battlefield between the forces of good
and evil (Rev. xvi. 16). North from the mouth of
Esdraelon, along the sea, runs the plain, sometimes
three or four miles wide, sometimes only just broad
enough to give a convenient passage, and once or
twice interrupted by headlands—on past Beirut and
Tripoli till we leave behind us the geographical limits
of Syria.

The *mountain system* is complex and bewildering
to a stranger. Surely there is no place of its size
elsewhere on the world's surface in which it is so easy
to lose one's way ! So many of the valleys look exactly
alike, and all are so tortuous, that as the present
writer has often experienced, the attempt to find a
short cut without a guide ends often in loss of time
and in unnecessary fatigue, even in the comparatively
simple southern portion. The mountains and valleys
of Samaria form a much more involved labyrinth than

those of Judaea. The two systems meet at a place called *Lebban*, roughly about the latitude of Jaffa.

In one respect the southern half of the mountain system differs from the northern. This is in the absence of sunken plains, surrounded completely by mountains and with little or no outlet. Such plains are found in the northern sections of the country, the most remarkable being *Merj el-Ghuruk*, on the direct line between Nablus and Jenin—and the plain called *el-Buttauf*, in the mountains of Galilee north of Esdraelon. These mountains may be said to possess the same perplexing character as those of Samaria to the south of the plain, though the valleys as a whole are wider, the hills less rugged, and owing to the greater wealth of springs there is more permanent vegetation throughout the year. The Judaean hills are intersected by valley systems, with elaborate ramifications and extremely tortuous, but all running definitely down to the maritime plain on the one hand and the Jordan valley on the other.

Seen from the coast plain, the Judaean mountains look like an impregnable wall, stretching continuously from north to south ; and when we scale this wall and stand in Jerusalem, on its summit, another wall is extended before us, seemingly yet more forbidding, as it is also even grander and more impressive. This is the so-called ' Mountains of Moab,' which, however, are not really mountains at all, but the edge of a lofty plateau that stretches eastward far into the desert, without a corresponding descent on the opposite side. This wall of rock, likewise, is broken by valleys, some of them, like the Mojib (Arnon), not to be matched for grandeur by anything on the western side, unless perhaps it be the Litany cañon at the point where the huge ruins of the Crusaders' castle of Belfort command it.

The Hauran, at the northern end of this East-Jordan land, is a great granary for the whole country. The southern part, well watered with rivers and with plentiful dew, is chiefly pasture-land, in places well wooded. Rich though Western Palestine is, the possibilities of Eastern Palestine are much higher; but the country is still, as it has been from the time of the earliest records, in the hands of unprogressive Bedawin, under whom development is impossible.

In a country of aspect so varied, it is natural that the climate should display many local varieties. All possible temperature from a cold almost arctic, to a heat little short of torrid, can be experienced within the compass of half a year. On the whole, however, the climate is agreeable, and with proper precaution, healthy. The year divides naturally into two seasons, the rainy and the dry: the former is apt to be broken, without warning, by torrential rains, though between the storms days of the most perfect beauty intervene: in the dry season rain falls only by the rarest and

most extraordinary exception, though heavy dews
make up for the want of moisture. The hot east wind
or *sirocco* makes life uncomfortable while it lasts—
often punishing undue expenditure of energy with
severe headaches. This wind is popularly supposed
to blow for three days at a time, though no such
regular rule is actually obeyed. Malaria, and the
manifold diseases that result from neglect or ignorance of sanitary laws, are the chief enemies of human
life in Palestine[1].

At a very remote date man must have made his
appearance in the land of Palestine. Rudely chipped
implements, of the Palaeolithic stage of culture, are
found in great numbers on the maritime plain, on the
summit of the Judaean mountains, on the uplands of
Moab, and in the caves of Phoenicia. Here and there
the writer has noticed chipped flints lying on the
ground while riding along the valleys of Samaria.

In the beginning of human life in the country,
man lived entirely on the products of the chase. He
was unacquainted with the arts of agriculture or the
domestication of animals, nor had he knowledge of
pottery-making, spinning or weaving. Clad, if at all,
in skins, he sheltered from the weather in booths of

---

[1] For statistics about population, climate, diseases, and other
details of the kind, on which within our limits it is impossible to
enlarge, reference should be made to the works cited in the classified
bibliography at the end of this book.

hide or of branches, or else in caves, of which the
limestone hills in Palestine present an ample choice.

Flint implements of the most primitive types, the
Chellean, and its later subdivision the Acheulean[1],
are common in Palestine wherever the remains of
Palaeolithic man have been found. Specimens of the
characteristic hand-axe have been picked up on the
maritime plain, in yet greater numbers on the plateau
south of Jerusalem, and in considerable quantities
in the region to the south of 'Amman, east of Jordan.
Some have also been discovered far to the south, in
the neighbourhood of Petra. It is significant that
none are yet reported from the lower reaches of the
Jordan valley—the explanation no doubt being that
in the Chellean period this was still occupied by the
Dead Sea, then much more extensive than in its
present shrunken dimensions. A magnificent collection of flint implements has been accumulated by the
Assumptionist Fathers of Notre-Dame de France, at
Jerusalem, and is stored in their excellent museum:
the publication of an illustrated catalogue of these
on the scale which the collection merits, would be a
benefit not only to Palestinian but also to Prehistoric
science.

[1] For an account of these periods of the Early Stone Age the
reader must be referred to special treatises, of which the fullest and
most thorough is Déchelette's *Manuel d'archéologie préhistorique,
celtique, et gallo-romaine*, Vol. I. (Paris, Picard, 1908). See also
Sollas, *Ancient Hunters* (Macmillan, 1911).

Palaeolithic man in Palestine missed, however, the higher developments attained by his brother in France. The former country has yielded nothing comparable with the splendid chipped flints of Solutré and its allied stations ; nor has the least trace of the exuberant art of the Magdalenian caves of the Pyrenees and elsewhere as yet come to light in the Holy Land[1].

The Mousterian type of flint scraper, which combines the efficiency of the early types with an economy of material, was the highest point attained by the Palestinians of the Early Stone Age. To this period belong the greater number of the cave settlements of Phoenicia, which have been explored with great scientific skill by Père Zumoffen of the University of Saint-Joseph, Beirut.

One of the Phoenician coast settlements belongs to the Magdalenian level of civilization[2]. This is the well-known cave of Antelias, in which were discovered fragments of a human skeleton—too small, unfortunately, to tell us much about its owner. He was a hunter, and in the *débris* on the floor of the cave were found many fragments of the bones of animals on which he had lived, as well as scrapers of

---

[1] The cave sculptures found at Gezer certainly belong to a later epoch.

[2] Perhaps this term would be better than "Period" as it avoids any hint of *absolute* limitation in time over the inhabited world.

flint resembling those assigned in Europe to the
Magdalenian level, though inferior in craftmanship to
the products of Magdalenian France. In this period
instruments of bone, such as prickers, begin to appear
in the deposits. They were used for sewing skins
together, for (as we have said) the hunter of the
Early Stone Age knew nothing of textile fabrics.

The latest writer on the stone age in Palestine,
Dr Max Blanckenhorn, has assigned the date 10,000
B.C. to the end of the Palaeolithic age and the beginning of the Neolithic. In estimating the probability
or otherwise of this calculation, it must not be forgotten that time has to be allowed, between the
Palaeolithic period and the late Neolithic as represented by the Gezer cave dwellers, for an earlier
Neolithic period, represented by some settlements in
Phoenicia, notably the cave of Harajel. Here sherds
of pottery were found—proving that we have reached
the Neolithic stage of culture—side by side with the
bones of extinct fauna, especially the woolly rhinoceros. This early Neolithic period is as yet but little
known—only a very few stations belonging to it have
been found: but the fact of its existence must not be
forgotten when endeavouring to calculate at what
time Palestine was first inhabited. The Gezer cave-
dwellers may roughly be assigned to 3000 B.C., so that
the dating of Dr Blanckenhorn is not unreasonable,
remembering that the first steps in civilization are

always the most difficult, and take a much longer time than the later phases. Of the beginning of the Palaeolithic period, or the length of its duration, we know absolutely nothing.

Fascinating though they be, we must not linger over these dim beginnings. With further exploration we may in time gain fuller knowledge about the first men who walked the sacred soil of Palestine. But we cannot hope that the corrosion of twelve thousand years will have left us more than a shadow of their memory.

CHAPTER II

THE LATER STONE AGE IN PALESTINE

In the course of the exploration of Gezer, under the auspices of the Palestine Exploration Fund, it was found that the rocky heart of the hill was full of caves, partly natural, partly artificial. These caves varied greatly in both size and plan. Some were mere cells or shelters, about eight to ten feet square; others were tortuous collections of chambers, united by doorways and passages. A flight of steps cut in the rock usually gave access to the floor; through the roof opening at the head of these steps came the only light that illuminated the cave. As a rule the roofs were low—a height of more than about seven feet being exceptional. In sifting the rubbish, with which the cave floors had become encumbered, it became evident that these holes in the rock had been the dwellings of a race of people of simple needs and of low culture. Rude pottery, made without the use of a potter's wheel, and ornamented with coarse moulding or roughly painted red lines; flint flakes, knives, and scrapers; millstones; rounded stone pebbles, that could be used for a variety of purposes—hearth stones, heating stones, missiles, polishers, etc.; perhaps an amulet or two of bone or of slate, perforated for suspension—these formed the furniture of the dwellings. Not a scrap of metal was found, save a few small fragments that had evidently washed in with the winter rains from the ruins of the later city, outside and above the cave mouths. No trace of evidence came to light, speaking of trade or converse with the great contemporary civilizations of the Euphrates or Nile valley.

In one cave some rude drawings scratched on the wall, representing cows and other animals, shewed a striving after art-expression such as manifests itself even in the lowest races. These were of infantile rudeness, and even the most successful could not for a moment compare with the extraordinary carvings and paintings of animal figures that the men of the

Fig. 1.   Graffiti in a cave found at Gezer.

Those here illustrated represent animals (the two uppermost standing
in long vegetation) and a human footprint.

reindeer age who inhabited the caves of France and Spain have bequeathed us.

These pictures tell us nothing of the life of the people who drew them, which we are obliged to infer as best we can from their caves and from the utensils they left behind them. These set before us an uncultured people, as yet unacquainted with metal, living by the chase and by their flocks, and by such simple agricultural processes as they had contrived. The poor character of their pottery, which is the chief relic of their handiwork, shews that they had not attained to so high a level of culture as had the Neolithic lake-dwellers of Europe. Spindle-whorls shewed that the art of spinning had been acquired by them, but as the soil and climate of Palestine have no preservative virtues—quite the reverse—their textile fabrics have of course totally disappeared.

One of the caves had evidently been used by this people as a place for the disposal of the dead. The body, placed at the sill of a chimney-aperture that provided a draught, was burnt: the remains becoming ultimately scattered and trampled over the whole surface of the floor. From one point of view this is unfortunate: the bones were too much destroyed by the action of the fire to make any very extensive examination of their ethnological character possible. All we can say is that we have to deal with a non-Semitic race, of *low* stature, with thick skulls, and

shewing evidence of the great muscular strength that
is essential to savage life.

Of their religion it is not possible to say much.
A space of rock in the middle of the city, covered
with cup-hollows and associated with curious caves,
into one of which was a drain as though for sacrificial
blood, may conceivably have been a place of sacrifice—
it is difficult to think of any other explanation that
will fit all the details so readily. But of the nature
of the rites that were observed at this place we have
no information whatever. Some pig-bones found in
the cave, at the bottom of the drain, may indicate
that the pig was a pre-Semitic sacrificial animal,
and may thus explain the horror of this creature
which has become traditional among the Semites.
But nothing more can be said of their religious
customs and beliefs—save that the presence of pottery
(no doubt originally containing food-offerings) in the
cremation cave shewed that they shared the universal
human belief in a life after death.

No other centres of population assignable to the
late Neolithic period have as yet been found in
Palestine, but there is every hope that with the
steady growth of interest in the exploration of the
mounds that dot its surface, further light will be
thrown upon it by future discoveries. Some other
relics of their handiwork however exist, in the
megalithic remains that are to be seen here and

there on both sides of the Jordan. Dolmens still abound in various parts of Eastern Palestine, and though few now remain west of the Jordan it is probable that there were formerly as many in the one division of the country as the other.

Some of the most remarkable Dolmen areas are those in the Jaulan and the Hauran, and are described by Schumacher[1], with illustrations of characteristic specimens. There are sometimes areas containing great numbers of these monuments—veritable pre-historic cemeteries. No scientific explorations of the contents have been made—that duty has been left to ignorant treasure-hunting Arabs—and we therefore know nothing of the details of the burials within them: but the coexistence at probably the same culture-level of the Gezer cremation cave, and the Moabite and Galilean dolmens, indicates that as in France the two chief methods of disposal of the bodies of the dead were used concurrently.

West of the Jordan, dolmens are confined to a few specimens in the district of Galilee, one near Abu Dis in the neighbourhood of Jerusalem, and two, one of them ruined, near Beit Jibrin, between Hebron and Gaza—the centre of that wonderful subterranean cave-city, which is one of the most baffling subjects that the Palestinian archaeologist can investigate.

[1] See *Across the Jordan*, p. 62 and *The Jaulan*, p. 123.

Many of the Moabite dolmens are surrounded by one or more rings of boulders. This is indeed a characteristic feature of the megalithic sepulchres of that region. Otherwise the circles of stones, so characteristic of various parts of Western Europe, do not occur. An example alleged to exist at Beitin (supposed to be the ancient Bethel) is probably a mere fortuitous arrangement, and not intentional. Single *menhirs* or standing stones do occur sporadically however: but whether these are to be considered as remains of the early period to which this chapter is devoted is doubtful, in view of the great importance of the standing stone in Semitic cultus. Cairns are found here and there, but offer no evidence of their date or purpose. There is a striking series on the hills south of Jerusalem which look like tumuli, but which have not been properly examined.

But probably the most remarkable prehistoric built monuments in the country are the series of five close to Hizmeh, a village a short distance north of Jerusalem, and locally known as the *Kabur Beni Isra'in*, 'the Graves of the Children of Israel.' These strange monuments consist of long broad walls, in one of which a chamber and a shaft have been made, happily compared by Père Vincent to an Egyptian *mastaba*[1]. A suggestion regarding these monuments was made some years ago by Clermont-Ganneau—

[1] Vincent, *Canaan*, p. 257.

Fig. 2.   One of the Kabûr Beni Isra'in.

The structure is roughly about 100 ft. long and 15 ft. broad.   The background offers a good
typical example of the rugged valley scenery in the Judaean mountains.

namely, that they are the basis of the tradition of Rachel's Tomb. This idea is simply thrown out by the way in Prof. Clermont-Ganneau's book[1], and so far as I know he has not yet returned to it, or given any attempt at demonstration. When the matter is looked into, it will be seen that though there are difficulties not easily got rid of, the theory is very probable.

How far the Biblical narrative preserves any traditions of the early pre-Semitic races is a very obscure question. We find many Palestinian tribes referred to, but there is really very little to shew whether the people named were Semitic or pre-Semitic, except such evidence as their place in history may afford. There are the Hivites, Perizzites, Jebusites, and the rest, so frequently enumerated in the story of the Exodus and the wanderings in the Wilderness: these, no doubt, were Semitic tribes, in race and language closely allied to the Hebrews themselves. The Amalekites, Midianites, and the rest of the trans-Jordanic tribes were certainly likewise Semitic, as much as their modern representatives, the Bedawin. It is, however, when we dig through this comparatively easy stratum that our difficulties begin. Underlying it we find people called Emim, Zamzummim, Zuzim, Rephaim, and Horites; we also find indications of a belief in

[1] *Archaeological Researches in Palestine*, Vol. II. p. 278.

people called Nephilim.   What are we to make of
these various ethnics?

The simplest and most probable answer to this
question is that we have in them traditions of actual
races, handed across the intervening Canaanitish
occupation, but mingled with current folklore to an
extent that the references to them in Hebrew literature are scarcely sufficient to enable us to gauge.
This is most clearly brought out in the case of the
Nephilim.   According to the record in Numbers xiii.
33, the spies when confronted with the tall people
who lived round Hebron, identified them with the
Nephilim, a race who according to a fragmentary
legend preserved in Genesis (vi. 1–4) had a half
human, half supernatural, ancestry.

Every people has traditions of predecessors in the
occupation of its country, which either as giants or
dwarfs figure in popular lore ; but there seems to be
reason for believing that in certain parts of Palestine
the invading Hebrews actually found a *tall* race
before them.   It is not necessary to postulate a *giant*
race ; there never has been such, anywhere.   If the
average stature of the aborigines were six inches or
so greater than the average stature of the invaders,
which is quite possible, that would be sufficient to
give birth to theories of a gigantic race.   The case of
the Patagonians, so long believed to be giants, affords
an exact parallel.   The average stature of this fine

people is about six feet; but the first travellers, un-
provided with such modern apparatus as pencils,
notebooks, and measuring tapes, and trusting over-
much to their memory—impressed also by single
individuals who happened to exceed the average—
brought back a report of them not unlike the report
of the 'Nephilim' which the spies brought back to
the anxious children of Israel.

This tall race, called more properly the Rephaim
or Anakim (whatever these names may mean[1]) seems
to have been established in the neighbourhood of
Hebron. A non-Semitic stock was apparently observed among the inhabitants of this district, and
vaguely termed 'the Hittites' by the author of
Gen. xxiii. 3—a name that is probably used simply
as a label for people recognised as being of alien race;
much as the names 'Fenish' (= Philistines) or 'Rum'
(= Greeks) are used by the fellahin of modern Palestine to denote ancient races to whom old buildings
and other relics are popularly ascribed. According to
the official history of the Hebrew immigration these
'giants' were driven out from Hebron by Joshua
(ch. xi. 21), and only a remnant was left in Gaza, Gath,
and Ashdod[2].

---

[1] Rephaim has the additional meaning 'ghosts' in Hebrew, an
accident which probably had some influence in investing the sons
of Anak with an uncanny reputation.

[2] Indicating that these places also were within their territory : it

Thus it appears that over Southern Palestine, from Hebron to Ashdod, there originally spread a tall non-Semitic race, who throughout the early Semitic occupation maintained their footing, and whose power was broken only by the Hebrew invaders. It is difficult to avoid connecting this people with the *origin* of the wonderful caves that are especially characteristic of just this part of the country. I especially emphasise the word *origin*, because there is clear evidence, in archways built of later masonry, in Christian and Muslim graffiti, and in other details, that the caves were used and modified in subsequent periods.

These caves consist of labyrinthine groups of square, rectangular, or circular chambers, hewn out of the soft limestone of the district with great care and exactness; they include water-stores, oil-presses, and other conveniences of life; and in fact are fully provided to be the residences, temporary or permanent, of families and groups of people. They vary greatly in size and complexity: one cave was found by the writer that contained no less than sixty chambers. This was quite exceptional: but caves with five, ten, or even twenty chambers, large and small, are not uncommon. The passages sometimes are so narrow as to make their exploration difficult; and the

is not said that they were driven from Hebron to settle in the cities named.

chambers are sometimes so large that it requires a bright light such as that of magnesium wire to illuminate them sufficiently for examination. One chamber, now fallen in, was found to have been 400 feet long and 80 feet high.

To have excavated these gigantic catacombs required the steady work of a long-settled population: it is unthinkable that they should have been made by fugitives, whether Christians avoiding persecution or Hebrews avoiding the Midianites—for it is highly probable that these are the 'dens in the mountains' referred to in Judges vi. 2, and said to have been made for such a purpose. Nor is it likely that these huge caves would have been cut out at all in *historic* times (*i.e.* after the settlement of the Hebrews) without some record or tradition attaching to them. At least, we can scarcely suppose that such immense engineering works would be undertaken unless required by a combination of historical circumstances to which some clue would be on record. We are driven back to conclude that the caves are the work of the race that, as we infer, inhabited just this district of Palestine, to whose fine physique the traditions about them bear testimony.

In the exact middle of the area bounded on one side by Hebron, and on the other by Gaza, Gath, and Ashdod, stands the village of Beit Jibrin, the 'House of Gabriel.' This is the great centre of the cave district. Close by stood in Hebrew times the town of Mareshah, apparently meaning 'the place at the head.' Later this name became Hellenised into *Marissa*, and it survives as Mer'ash, the name of a ruined village of the Roman period. The town was destroyed in B.C. 40; but sometime before A.D. 68 it was refounded as *Baitogabra*, which is the origin of the modern corruption. Now *Baitogabra* does not mean 'House of Gabriel.' It is very probable that this is really an ancient name that has risen to the surface from the depths of the popular memory, and that it represents an ancient *Bêth ha-gibbôrim*, 'House of the Mighty Men'—a memory of the Rephaite race that once inhabited the district of which it is the centre.

North of the Rephaim were apparently the puny and much less civilized Gezerite cave-dwellers. East of the Jordan were similar tribes—the Emim or 'dreadful ones,' the Zamzummim or Zuzim[1], apparently 'murmurers' or 'stammerers,' *i.e.* 'speakers of a barbarous tongue'—and east of the Jordan are found caves similar to those of Beit Jibrin (notably at ed-Der'a); but nowhere do they occur in such numbers or magnitude.

It should be noted that though the Gezerite cave-

---

[1] It is generally believed that one of these names is erroneous, being a scribal error or misreading for the other, and that one tribe is denoted by both.

dwellers were still in the stone age, the hewers of the Beit Jibrin caves possessed the use of metal tools, as the pick-marks testify. The cave-dwellers, therefore, fall into the overlap of stone and bronze. Perhaps the small race at Gezer were an earlier stock that would ultimately have been driven out altogether by the Rephaim if the Semitic invasion had not checked the progress of the latter. But here we trespass on the perilous quag of conjecture.

CHAPTER III

THE PRE-ISRAELITE SEMITIC OCCUPATIONS

In the heart of the ancient world, bridging together Asia and Africa, yet cut off almost completely from both by tongues of sea and by desert wastes, lies the vast, inscrutable land of Arabia. Closed to explorers by its own difficulties, by the wildness of its tribes, and by the fanatical exclusiveness that still centres round the ancient cult of the Black Stone, it still remains one of the least known regions on the surface of the globe, in spite of intrepid attempts during the past century to open up its secrets.

Inscrutable as itself are the people whose home it is. Whence the Semites originally came is a question whose answer lies hidden in the mists of ages. But it is on the assumption of an Arabian centre of distribution that the various phenomena of the peopling of the nearer East can most easily be explained. For though Arabia may breed vast numbers of its nomad tribes it cannot support them: and though the struggle for existence may be diminished artificially by the inhabitants, by means of intertribal battles and, in ancient times, of infanticide, yet a time comes periodically when necessity forces its surplus population to overrun the more fertile neighbouring lands. The country, as it has been noticed, comes into prominence historically every thousand years, more or less. Within the first decade of the twentieth century, the Turkish government had the gravest difficulty in quelling insurrections of the Bedawin in the province of Yaman: most likely this was ultimately due to the cause which produced the great semi-military, semi-religious movement in the seventh century, of which Muhammad was the central figure —the Nabataean outbreaks, in the fourth and fifth centuries B.C.—the tribal movements of which the Exodus was an episode, about 1200 B.C.—the earliest Semitic outbursts on Palestine, which must have been from 2000 to 2500 B.C.—and the yet earlier invasions by which the first Semitic colonists established themselves in the rich plains of Mesopotamia.

Portraits of Assyrian kings, and of Semitic captives in Egypt, preserve for us the likeness of members of

the various tribes and sub-tribes which may be said
to have come into being by these successive migra-
tions. They illustrate the closeness of the Semitic
unity: the type of features, familiar to all if only
from modern caricatures of contemporary Jews, per-
sists throughout, and is sufficient to tell us that,
various though the fortunes of Babylonians and
Bedawin, Hebrews and Phoenicians, Assyrians and
Amorites, may have been, yet they were all one
people, united, whether they would admit it or not,
by the closest bonds of blood-brotherhood. The
evidence of language supports the evidence of physio-
gnomy. As compared with the wide morphological
differences between Aryan tongues, the Semitic
languages seem but dialects of a common speech, so
nearly do they resemble one another both in gram-
matical structure and in vocabulary.

The earliest of the Semitic colonizations that we
can trace are the Babylonian, in the regions of the
Euphrates. When this powerful people and the
Assyrians were once established there, they blocked
further progress eastward: future outbursts were
diverted toward the west, and compelled to seek a
home in the lands bordering on the Mediterranean.

The report of the spies, which we have already
had occasion to allude to in connexion with the giant
race, graphically illustrates the appeal which the
richness of the land of Palestine made to eyes

atrophied by the barren desert. The fatuous (not to say profane) popular notion that the land is blighted by a Divine curse, is an index of a deplorable want of imagination. The promise of 'a land flowing with milk and honey' was not made to a crowd of beef-fed excursionists, coming from cultivated and developed lands of the modern West, but to tribes of half-starved wanderers, fighting their way from oasis to oasis over sterile sands.

This first Semitic immigration never found its historian. Its leaders and their deeds are forgotten. Probably it was not essentially different in character from the immigrations that followed it. Though so close in kin, there is strangely little cohesion in the Semitic body ; tribes break away from one another on small occasion, and often become hostile to one another. So the Habiru and the Sutu came in the fifteenth century: so, later, came Judah and Ephraim: so, in the Arab immigration, came Yaman and Kais. And as all these fell apart from time to time, or actually went to war with one another, we may assume that probably the first Semitic immigration was a congeries of closely related but loosely united tribes. In one respect the invasion differed from any that came after it, namely in the non-Semitic character of the defeated races. The Semites, armed as they were at least to some extent with bronze weapons, had the advantage over them, and at any rate partially

succeeded in wresting the land from them. They left
the formidable Rephaim alone, as the Hebrews found
this people still in possession when they arrived. The
more insignificant people whose remains were found
at Gezer were apparently annihilated. Indeed it is
at Gezer that the chief indications of the First Semitic
Invasion were discovered.

In two important respects the First Semitic invaders were superior, as regards their civilization, to
the people they dispossessed—namely, in the use of
bronze, as just mentioned, and in the use of a simple
form of potter's wheel. Otherwise they cannot be
said to have been much in advance of their predecessors. At first they lived in the caves that these
had been obliged to vacate, but before long they
began to build houses, of the type that has persisted,
with wonderfully little change, down to the villages
of modern twentieth century Palestine. It consists
of an open courtyard, where most of the domestic
work is done during the day, and of a number of
small rooms that serve as stables, store-rooms and
sleeping chambers. These invaders no doubt brought
with them their particular variety of the Semitic cults
which, again, are in their natural shape of sufficiently
uniform character to demonstrate the close connexion
between the members of the Semitic race. Probably
they began to rear pillars, one of the chief tangible
expressions of Semitic worship. They never imitated

their predecessors by burning the dead—this practice is repugnant to all Semites—but they flung them carelessly into a cave, where they were left as they fell.

Some time about 2000 to 1800 B.C.—in the absence of records it is impossible to fix the date more definitely—we find a rather sudden advance in civilization to have taken place. This, like all the other forward steps of which recent excavation in the country has revealed the traces, was due to foreign interference. The Semitic natives, Amorite, Hebrew, or Arab, never invented anything: they assimilated all the elements of their civilization from without. This principle is the key to the interpretation of all remains of antiquity found in the land of Palestine. If we pass through the successive strata of an ancient town, as laid bare by the explorer's spade, we can perceive a foreign stimulus powerfully affecting the whole culture at some particular stage of history. Then in succeeding generations we can trace the influence gradually deteriorating, till, just when it is about to disappear altogether, it is swamped by fresh influences from somewhere else. Egypt first; then those great civilizations of Crete and the Aegean, that have slumbered forgotten till waked to life again in our own days, but whose influence lasts through practically the whole history of Palestine as covered by the Old Testament. Then, in quick succession,

follow the Classical Greek culture, Rome, and Byzantium : then Muhammadanism in the vigour of its
fresh youth : then the extraordinary attempt to graft
West European feudalism on the country, which we
call the Crusades. After the fall of the Latin kingdom
the culture of the country collapses into an almost
recordless semi-barbarism, till new ideas, new
machinery, and, above all, new colonists from Europe
have within the last century quickened it once more
to life.

From first to last there was not a native potter
in Palestine who could so much as invent a new
design to paint on his waterpots. There was not an
armourer who could invent a new pattern of sword
or arrowhead. The modern peasants live in houses
practically identical in style and construction with
those which sheltered the peasants of 2000 B.C.—a
community of white ants could not be more unprogressive. It is the last country in the world,
perhaps, where it would be natural for us to expect
the development of an original conception of divinity
so totally at variance with the ' gods of the nations '
as that which we find in the writings of the Hebrew
prophets.

Towards the beginning of the third millennium
B.C. we have very definite claims made by Lugalzaggizi,
king of Lagash, to domination over all the lands
from the Persian gulf to what is supposed to be the

Mediterranean Sea. But as yet no trace of this very ancient domination has been found in the country itself: some lucky explorer of the future may find relics that will speak of it. Meanwhile, the oldest foreign civilization of whose influences definite relics have come to light within the land of Palestine, is that of Egypt under the twelfth dynasty.

The absence of any Egyptian inscriptions recording conquest in the country, makes it probable that this influence was commercial rather than military. The history of the relations of Egypt and Palestine during this period is very little known. The large number of scarabs, amulets, and personal adornments bearing hieroglyphic inscriptions or decorations referable to the twelfth dynasty, which have been found (especially at Gezer) is evidence of the importance of the influence exercised at the time by Egyptian culture.

Perhaps the best way of forming an idea of Palestinian culture, when the influence of twelfth dynasty Egypt was playing upon it, would be to enter in thought into a city of the period, and try to conjure up a vision of what we should see. The recently excavated city of Gezer may be chosen as the basis of our imaginings, but the description would in general fit any other city of its time.

Rather, let us first take our stand on the hill-top to the south, now crowned by a modern Muslim shrine which, perhaps, represents an ancient holy place: and

let us look at the scene below. The long narrow hill
once crowned by the ancient city is now deserted,
save for a house built by European land-owners some
forty years ago. Between the ancient site and our
standpoint is the flat stretch of bare rock that is
used as the threshing-floor of the village. To the
left of the threshing-floor is the modern village, the
evil odour of which taints the air for a considerable
radius outside its own borders. The village streets are
narrow, crooked, and unclean. The houses are built
of rough stones, set in mud, and are plastered with the
same material: here and there attempts at decoration,
with crude painted geometrical patterns, are to be
noticed. The roofs are flat: the rooms are two or
three in number, devoid of all but the most essential
furniture. Human beings and animals herd together
at night, the former being at most separated from
the latter by being on a raised platform. Offensive
insects infest every corner. A few melancholy-
looking dogs prowl about seeking what they may
devour.

The people live just the life that might be
expected under such unhealthy conditions. The
young children are peculiarly evil-looking morsels of
humanity, and are not bettered by their distended
paunches, the result of unrestrained water-drinking.
As they grow older their appearance improves, and
some of the young men of about 20 are decidedly

Fig. 3. A CORNER OF A PALESTINIAN VILLAGE.

The houses on the left are typical, and illustrate the description in the text. On the right are piles of straw stored for fodder, fuel, etc., and plastered with mud and manure to protect them from the weather.

fine looking, though there are many others who are less attractive. Some of the women are not uncomely at about the age of 15 or 16, but they rapidly deteriorate after this time, and age very early. Old women are much rarer than old men: but in both sexes it is still true that threescore and ten is the highest possible limit of age to which an average person can hope to attain.

Now as we stand by the Muslim shrine, let us draw back the curtain of the past, and imagine ourselves in the time of the last kings of the twelfth dynasty.

The little modern village to the left is swept out of existence at once. The silent ridge before us, on the other hand, becomes alive with a large city, about half a mile in length, surrounded by a colossal wall which is broken at intervals by shallow projecting towers. This wall probably stands 20 or 30 feet above the ground and is about 14 feet thick. The top is protected by a breast-high parapet, from over which missiles can be cast down by the defenders on a besieging army. But the time of storm and stress for Gezer, so far as it is recorded for us in written history, is not yet.

In the wall facing us, a little west of the middle, is a gate of the city—a narrow entrance flanked by two massive towers of brick. How this entrance was closed there is not sufficient evidence to shew:

it is possible that two portcullis-like diaphragms of wood were dropped into the spaces between six great slabs of stone, three on each side, and these wedged up with baulks of timber. But this is mere conjecture.

Passing through the gate, which is paved with cobble-stones polished smooth by footwear, we find ourselves in a scene that almost reproduces the sight of the modern village with which we filled our eyes before plunging into the past. We see narrow, crooked, unclean streets. Our nostrils are assailed by the stench of an airless, drainless oriental town. We see stone houses set in mud, plastered in mud, with one story, flat roofs, and courtyards inside, with raised platforms for sleeping—in fact we see just such houses as we saw in the modern village. We see the same unhealthy people, the same insects, the same dogs. In essential particulars the life of to-day is the same as the life of three and a half millennia back. Here is a knot of children, all of them wearing conspicuously some kind of amulet to avert the still-dreaded evil eye, and probably very little else. There at some shop-keeper's stall a quarrel is raging over a false weight, such as we might hear any day in the village ; and, allowing for dialectic differences, many of the violent expressions of abuse that we may overhear are identical with those that are still indulged in during these short

and stormy scenes. If we return a half hour later
we shall very likely find that the combatants have
by some mysterious influence become reconciled,
and are playing some game like draughts together.

But we are still at the gate of the city. Let us
penetrate a little further in, and let us as we do so
look out for those points of contrast which record
the development of civilization.

Of course the first and most obvious difference
between the past and the present is the difference
of religion, and all that religion involves or implies.
Our city is destined to be subject in turn to the
influence of Philistines, bringing their exotic culture
and cultus from oversea; of Hebrews, gradually
sloughing off the nature-worship they have inherited
from their Semitic ancestors, and developing their
sublime monotheism; of Assyrian and of Greek
paganism; of Maccabean puritanism; of Eastern
Christianity, under the Byzantine Empire; of
Muhammadanism; of Western Christianity, under
the Crusades; and of Muhammadanism restored,
which has now exercised its influence for seven
unbroken centuries. A greater contrast could not
well be imagined between the official religions in
the ancient Canaanite city and in the modern Arab
village.

Though deity was localised, according to early
Semitic theory, so that an exile was obliged to

'serve other gods' when driven to another country,
we should unquestionably find a synthesis of religions
in this ancient city. The Egyptian residents especially seem to have brought their gods with them:
and (as moulds for producing impressions testified)
figures of Egyptian divinities were modelled locally.
There was probably a temple to some Egyptian
divinity in the city, which, however, was totally
destroyed, only one stone with a hieroglyphic letter
remaining to speak of a building inscribed all over
like the temples of the Nile valley. This, however,
was at a later date than that with which we are at
present concerned. The native Semites continued
their cult of the local *numen*, a being to be propitiated by sacrifices of the most terrible kind, and
of the great Mother-goddess of whom crude representations came to light by scores in the course of
the excavation.

These ancient deities are not yet wholly dead.
They survive in the cult of the local shrines such
as that by which we took our stand when beginning
this our attempt to peer into the past. There is not
a landscape in Palestine which is not dominated by
one of the white-domed hill-top sanctuaries, now
dedicated to the memory of some true-believing
Muslim who acquired sanctity in one way or another,
but notwithstanding still carrying on, under a thin
disguise, the traditions of the primitive Semitic

hill-top shrines. The High Places have not even yet
been taken away. And, as has been said so often that
it is now a mere commonplace, the oath by the sheikh
is far more binding locally than an oath by the
Supreme Being. Within sight of Gezer is the shrine
of the Sheikh Selman. Accuse a man of theft, and
he will swear by Allah to his innocence in the most
emphatic way. Conduct him to Sheikh Selman and
ask him to place his hand on the tomb and then to
take an oath of compurgation—it will not be difficult
to discover the truth from his behaviour under such
an ordeal.

If we turn to the left on passing through the gate
we shall come to a work which it is impossible to
imagine the modern natives executing. This is the
tunnel of Gezer, whereby for some five hundred
years the city was provided with a copious supply
of water inside the walls. The advantage of this in
siege-time needs no pointing out. But who it was
that designed this grandiose excavation, by what
means and for how long the work was carried on,
and what was its original purpose, are questions that
cannot now be answered.

A few words of description may be given of this
great engineering work, as, to say the least, it must
considerably increase our respect for the Canaanite
civilization to contemplate it. It is a passage,
12 feet across and 23 feet high at the top—a little

less at the bottom—sloping downward at an angle
of about 30 degrees, with a staircase of eighty steps,
to a depth of over 90 feet vertically below the
surface of the rock. The whole work was executed
by means of tools of flint. At the bottom of the
tunnel is a vast natural cave, with no outlet—a
pocket in the heart of the rock. Here rises a powerful spring of water.

Thus, the ancient Canaanite population here executed a work which would no longer be possible to
their degenerate descendants. These found the work
of clearing out the mere loose stones and earth with
which the tunnel had become filled a sufficient tax
on their strength. In various parts of the country
—notably at Bittir, near Jerusalem—there are small
passages which have been cut in the rock in order
to direct the water of a spring to a convenient spot.
These are of Roman workmanship. Also no doubt
Roman are the splendidly built wells, one in almost
every village, from which the water supply of the
community is still drawn. The modern fellahin have
entered on the inheritance of these ancient works,
but are quite incapable of matching them.

Let us make our way further through the city.
Here we find a hole in the ground, stopped by a
great stone. It is the entrance—one of several
entrances—to a huge cave, once a residence of the
cave-dwellers that were driven out some few hundreds

of years before; but now adapted as a cemetery
by a wealthy family whose members are there buried,
with their treasures.

Turning to the right and wandering eastwards
through crooked lanes, we find ourselves at last just
about the middle of the city, and standing in an open
square. This is the High Place, the centre of the
City's religious life. The High Place of Gezer has by
now been so often described that it would be super-
fluous to expend space in an account of it here.
And of the rites enacted there, it is impossible to
better the account of one who, if not an eye-witness,
was sufficiently near to them to have full knowledge
of their nature: it will be found in Isaiah lvii. 5–6.

Let us resume our walk through the city, and
pause to watch this potter at work. The new make
of potter's wheel has recently been introduced: his
predecessors in the trade had to form the vessel with
one hand, rotating the wheel with the other. As the
potter we see plies his trade, he can with the improved instrument sit and rotate it with his foot,
leaving both hands free for modelling. The result is
that his vessels are much better made than was the
case two or three centuries ago: but this is also due
to his having better models to follow. Before his
eyes are fine vessels that merchants have brought
from Egypt, and yet finer works of art that have
been carried from an island of the sea which he

knows as Alashia, but which we call Cyprus—whither
their art has come from the lands of great and
mysterious sea-kings of whom he possibly knows by
vague hearsay. And he is spending his life in the
little cell where we find him, modelling feeble copies
of these ceramic masterpieces, and painting feeble
copies of their coloured decoration on his handiwork.

Next door is another craftsman. He is a worker
in flint—for though bronze has now been in use
for a considerable time, the old material is still
employed for rough work, and for purposes for which
bronze is not hard enough or too expensive. Rock
is quarried with flint: wheat is reaped with flint
sickles: the skins of slaughtered animals are scraped
clean with flint: this tradesman finds plenty of custom
as he sits and splinters flakes off the nodules that
are found in abundance in the chalky hills around.
A century or two later his descendants engaged in
the same trade will be startled to hear of an Egyptian
who has come with two axe-heads made of a material
that he calls something like *ba-en-pet*, the 'metal of
heaven'—for it falls from time to time from the blue
vault of heaven, which must therefore be made of
this material. It is harder than the hardest bronze,
and for weapons and agricultural and carpenter's
tools is of marvellous efficiency! But the Egyptian
is fated to have the misfortune to lose his precious
axe-heads in the water-tunnel, where they lay till

the excavators found them; and the menace to the
flint trade will be postponed for another five hundred
years. For it will not be till 1000 B.C. that iron is
destined to come into general use, and not till then
will flint be finally abandoned for such purposes as
have been named above.

Here next is a carpenter and joiner, working with
tools of bronze and bone, and like the potter, feebly
imitating Egyptian models. Then comes a weaver,
and then perhaps a goldsmith. A shrewd man of
business is this goldsmith, with two drawers-full of
little stone weights: the one lot too light, to sell
with; the other lot too heavy, to buy with[1]. And he
too is turning out from his moulds by the gross
copies of ear-rings and amulets such as are worn in
Egypt, and never thinks of trying to strike out on an
original line of his own.

And so the busy life goes on in the town. Of
course, like all orientals, ancient and modern, the
people pass their time in the fear of the caprice of
their deity and of their despot, who lives in that large
building we passed on the right in entering the city
gate—a building which was as plain as the rest, and

[1] A weight which is a correct multiple of any standard is one of
the rarest things that an excavator in the East can discover. Loss
by wear or injury has always to be allowed for, but this will not
account for all the deviations from accuracy; nor of course will it
explain the weights that are *in excess* of their proper amount.

only distinguished from its companions by its superior
size, so that it was not worth our while to stop to
give it closer examination.   In the courtyard of the
building was sunk the shaft of the colossal tunnel.

But in spite of despot or deity the people seem
fairly contented and prosperous.   Perhaps it was
the happiest time in the whole history of Gezer.
The fertile lands of the city produced an abundant
harvest.   The olive-groves—far more extensive than
the poor remnant of to-day—filled the rock-cut
vats with oil.   There were riches in the city
and men and walls to defend them, and the people
ate and drank, married and gave in marriage, and
bought and sold, and lived secure, without thought
of what a day would bring forth.

The security for a time seemed justified.   They
might occasionally feel a passing twinge of appre-
hension of a raid by Bedawin or by Egyptians.   But
the apprehensions would be allayed soon after the
time of our walk through the city.   For the Bedawin
found the outlet they needed in Egypt itself.   As a
tidal wave sweeps all before it, so the Bedawin burst
on Egypt and, sweeping away the glories of the
middle empire, established the rule of the 'shepherd
kings' that dominated the land for some two
hundred years.   While these savages had the wealth
of Egypt to fatten upon, they had no need to turn
aside to the less inviting pastures of Palestine:

while the blood of Egypt was being sucked it had no
strength for foreign aggression. So the life of the
Palestinian city went on happily enough, and the
only change we can trace is, as might be expected, a
steady increase in the amount of direct or indirect
Cretan influence on its civilization, and a corresponding decrease in that of Egypt.

Let us suffer four hundred years to pass by and
once more walk through the city.

There is a new and stronger wall now. The
houses we saw in our first visit have all gone, and
their places are taken by others of the same style.
The potter, the weaver, the goldsmith, the carpenter
still ply their trade as of old, and still turn out
shoddy imitations of foreign goods as of old: a
little different in style—on the whole inferior, both
in design and execution—but essentially the same as
before.

But I think we might notice a subtle change in
the bearing and manner of the people. For the city
has passed through a succession of vicissitudes.
First the hero Ahmose had arisen and helped Egypt
to shake off the yoke of foreign barbarians: then the
still greater Thutmose III had expanded the empire
by force of arms, and Palestine and Syria had fallen
under his rule. What might have been had his

successors been men of his calibre, with hands strong
to retain the empire he had won for them, it is
futile to speculate. For this was not to be. Amen-
Hotep III was a worthy successor of the great
Thutmose : but he is dead, and on his throne sits an
aesthete and dreamer, who spends his time developing
his theories of religion and of art, and ignores the
weighty affairs of empire. And the Bedawin, driven
back on their deserts, who must perforce find an outlet where they may, are pressing down on Palestine.

One Yapakhi sits in the governor's seat in the
city. We know nothing of him but what we can
glean from the four short letters written by him to
the heedless dilettante, his overlord to whom he was
obliged to give lip-service : and no one can be
expected to look his best when so engaged, particu-
larly when he is begging for assistance that never
comes, against enemies rapidly increasing in strength,
and is moreover distracted by dissensions in his own
household. His brother joined himself to the Bedawin, as did almost all the princes of Palestine one
by one, despairing of support from the egregious
Akhnaton. One town after another falls before the
invaders, and at last, headed (as it would appear) by
one Beia, son of Gulati, they invest Gezer itself, and it
becomes their prey. The inhabitants accepted the
inevitable with an equanimity we can hardly blame
under the circumstances. They threw themselves

whole-heartedly into the cause of the Bedawin, and
helped them with provisions and men when they
were engaged in their operations against the citadel
of Jerusalem, which in the face of every discouragement long remained attached to the Egyptian king
with a loyalty worthy of a better object.

These distractions cannot but have had a demoralising effect on the civilization of the country.
We can trace its influence in the decline everywhere
apparent in the standard of art, such as it was.   The
artificial unity produced by the Egyptian overlord-
ship, if indeed a unity ever existed, falls to pieces,
and the whole country becomes a mass of little
clans, scarcely more than a collection of independent villages, with such highly developed mutual
jealousy that union for a common purpose, even for
the public safety, was out of the question.   The
Canaanite civilization was in fact falling into a hopeless decline, when the next great raids on Palestine
took place.

CHAPTER IV

THE FIRST STRUGGLE OF WEST AND EAST

WE began the last chapter with a glance at Arabia
and the East-lands.   Now we must turn our eyes for
a moment to the West, where for long years events

had been preparing the way for the next scene of our drama.

From an immemorial antiquity the island of Crete, fortified by her navies that commanded the Eastern Mediterranean, and that rendered possible a mutually advantageous trade with Egypt, had been advancing forward by rapid steps along the road of culture, till it developed what was perhaps the highest and, in many respects, the most modern civilization that the ancient world ever saw. To follow the stages of the wonderful history of this island, as recent excavations have revealed it, is an absorbing task, but it would be both impossible and out of place in the present pages. We may take the glories of the palace of Cnossos for granted, noting only that the triumphs of the Cretan artificers afforded models for the efforts of the Palestinian craftsmen.

It is, however, important for us to notice, that much about the time when the Bedawin tribes were vexing the souls of the petty chieftains of the Amorites, as we described at the end of the previous chapter, the great Cretan civilization received its death-blow. The island was sacked, and its people dispersed to various parts of the Aegean and the south coasts of Asia Minor, carrying with them traditions of their ancient maritime prowess and of their achievements in the field of art, but too much broken up to attain again the heights that they had reached in the days of their prosperity.

The various branches of the dispersion of the Cretans, shortly after the sack of their native land, begin to make their appearance on the Egyptian monuments, which display them in a sinister light. Their piracies give trouble to the Egyptian fleets. They league themselves with the foes of Egypt, and are with difficulty beaten back. They seriously interfere with the comfort of the great Hittite empire, and overrun its outposts in N. Syria. Finally, in the reign of Ramessu III, they prepare a great expedition to descend on Egypt both by land and by sea. But Ramessu, the last great king of Egypt, was equal to the occasion. Having already thoroughly organized the military resources of Egypt, he beat the invaders back from his coasts. The 'Peoples of the Sea' met with a severe repulse at his hands, and were compelled to fall back on lands outside the dominion of the conquering Pharaoh.

The nearest and most convenient land for them was the coast-line of Palestine, and here the remnant of the invaders established themselves—at first towards the north, but gradually creeping southward as the strength of Egypt waned, under the feeble kings that succeeded Ramessu III.

On the Egyptian monuments the chief tribe among the 'Peoples of the Sea' is called *Purasati*, which name, there can be no doubt, is to be equated to the familiar *Philistines* of the Old Testament.

Fig. 4. A Philistine Captive.
One of the wall-carvings in the temple of Ramessu III at
Medinet Habu.

4—2

Thus the Westerns first came in contact with the land of Palestine. Though severely crippled by their losses in their fatal battle with the Egyptians, they would probably have been equal to wiping out the decaying Semitic communities, had not an access of new blood, with eager national aspirations, been already infused into the latter. Three important tribes, the Kenites, Judah, and Ephraim, with a number of subordinate septs, had crossed the Jordan and had begun a systematic attempt to colonize the country.

This invasion was different from any that had gone before. Strange happenings and strange covenants had linked these tribes together in a strong religious brotherhood. Some, at any rate, of their number had come up from servitude in Egypt, and their adventures coloured in time the traditions of the whole community. Judah and the Kenites, with the subordinate Simeonites, turned towards the south and overran the whole district of Hebron. Ephraim and its satellite clans made their way towards the north, and occupied certain districts from the ancient sanctuary of Bethel northward. But on many important cities they made no impression: the fertile coast plain it was out of their power to capture, and between the two branches of the invasion stood unconquered the citadel of Jerusalem, keeping them apart.

The newcomers were not made welcome by the nations round about. Moabites, Canaanites, Midianites, tribes of the same stock as themselves, in turn endeavoured to dispossess them and, according to the native traditions, succeeded in imposing upon them some kind of serfdom or vassalage. They had not yet attained to the conception of a central monarchy; but as occasion arose a popular leader was found in this tribe or that, who successfully championed his people against their oppressors.

It must have been when matters were in this state that the Philistine raid on Egypt, its repulse, and the subsequent settlement on the Palestinian coast took place. This introduced many complications into Palestinian politics: though its ultimate result was wholly beneficial to the Hebrew people. It gave the necessary pressure that unified them, so far as they could be unified into one nation: and it held up an ideal of civilization before their barbarous eyes which must have been a stimulus to their ambition, however they may have affected to despise their rivals.

The Philistines' settlement originally extended far beyond the region allowed them in the current Bible maps. In Egyptian records we find them established at Dor, south of Carmel. The story of the great battle of Gilboa, and the subsequent events, shew that they must have commanded the plains of Esdraelon, and consequently, even so late as the end of the reign of Saul, must have held the coast north of Carmel: the far inland town of Beth-Shan—which was situated close to the Jordan—was then evidently in their hands.

This first struggle of West and East in Palestine was a curious reversal of the usual circumstances of such antagonisms. We are inclined to picture the West as a thing of yesterday, new-fangled with its inventions and its progressive civilization; and the East as an embodiment of hoary and unchanging tradition. But when West first met East on the shores of the Holy Land, it was the former which represented the magnificent traditions of the past, and the latter which looked forward to the future. The Philistines were of the remnant of the dying glories of Crete: the Hebrews had no past to speak of, but were entering on the heritage they regarded as theirs, by right of a recently ratified divine covenant.

At first, however, the Philistines had their will of country and people. The Samson epic, which concentrates into the person of a single champion the events of a border guerilla warfare—the slaughtering of bands of the enemy with rude and extemporised weapons, the burning of crops, and so forth—postulates a background of passive subjection on the part of the Hebrews to their Western conquerors. The struggle in the following century was long and severe. The sheikhs of the Hebrews could do little in formal warfare against their warlike enemies ; they tried to make up for their military deficiencies by bringing the Ark into battle, with disastrous results. Without a ruler capable of organization, the scattered and divided tribes of Israel could never have rid themselves unaided of the Philistine yoke.

Such a leader was found at first in Samuel, whose official position in the sanctuary at Shiloh gave a religious sanction to his work. But as Samuel advanced in years he became more and more absorbed in his religious duties, and there was good reason to fear that the sons he would leave behind would not follow worthily in his steps. It became clear that a leader who should devote himself entirely to the duty of conducting the people to war was an absolute necessity if the Hebrews were to continue to exist. A young Benjamite, distinguished among other things by his physical excellence, was selected. The traditions vary as to whether Samuel resented or accepted without demur this encroachment on his judicial functions—he certainly strongly resented a subsequent trespass on his priestly privileges by the newly-appointed king. However, Samuel anointed him, and his reign, inaugurated by his brilliant delivery of Jabesh-Gilead, promised happily for the oppressed and suffering people. But the high hopes were doomed to disappointment : symptoms of mental derangement made their appearance, probably early in his career, manifesting themselves in a tendency to melancholia and to an unhealthy religious excitement. The malady was unquestionably aggravated by the treatment the unhappy king suffered at the hands of Samuel—amounting virtually to what would now be called excommunication—and by the bitterness of seeing his own prowess and popularity waning before that of his young armour-bearer, whose extraordinary influence over his son and heir-apparent was no doubt a further perpetual irritation. And perhaps the deepest tragedy lies in this, that his mournful story has been recorded for all time by a writer who was entirely out of sympathy with him. So far from leading his people to victory, the poor insane king, when he and his house were swept out of existence at Gilboa, left the Philistines stronger than they had ever been before.

The complete reversal of the situation under David is a very remarkable historical phenomenon. At first the successor of Saul reigned over the southern division of the Hebrew kingdom, probably by grace of the Philistines of whom he had, during his exile, become a vassal. But when he captured the Jebusite stronghold of Jerusalem, and united the northern kingdom with the southern, the Philistines came up against a rival who was thus making himself too

powerful. Three combats with the Philistines are
recorded, after which the Philistines seem to have
collapsed suddenly and for ever. Even the revolt of
Absalom did not encourage them to take the opportunity of attempting to regain their lost ground. From
this point onwards, the Philistines gradually became
absorbed in their Semitic surroundings. Down to
the time of Nehemiah their language lingered in the
town of Ashdod (Neh. xiii. 24); but probably this was
the last relic of their nationality that was preserved.

Such was, in outline, the course of the struggle
when first West met East in Palestine. Remembering
that we are writing a history not of events but of
civilization in the country, it is time to enquire in
what state was culture while this conflict was
going on.

There were three elements which we have to take
into account at the beginning of the struggle. There
was the now decaying civilization of the sedentary
Canaanites, in their cities 'with walls reaching up to
heaven' as the alarmed spies reported. It can hardly
be claimed that anything was contributed by the
immigrant nomads who overran the country; an
abrupt deterioration of all the arts is the only result
that could be expected from this barbarian influx.
On the other hand, the cultured Philistines to some
extent restored the balance, and from this point of
view it was a most fortunate circumstance that they

so completely dominated the country at the early formative period of the history of the Hebrew nation. Had it not been for this fact, the clock might have been put a long way back, and the land sunk into a barbarism from which it would have taken many centuries to emerge.

The only contributions the Hebrews made to the culture of the country were their simple desert customs and their religious organization. On the other hand, the Philistines, sprung from one of the great homes of art of the ancient world, had brought with them the artistic instincts of their race : decayed no doubt, but still superior to anything that was to be met with among the works, in stone, pottery, or metal, of the native Semitic craftsmen of the country. The Philistines, in fact, were the only cultured or artistic race who ever occupied the soil of Palestine, at least until the time when the influence of classical Greece asserted itself too strongly to be withstood. Whatsoever things raised life in the country above the dull animal existence of fellahin were due to this people. Palestine was in very truth the land of the Philistines, as its name declares unto this day ; and the peasantry of the modern villages— who care almost as little as their cattle for the history of the land they inhabit—still tell of the great days of old when it was inhabited by the mighty race of the ' Fenish.'

The history recorded in the Book of Judges gives us a picture of almost complete savagery, without laws, without organization, when every man did what was right in his own eyes. In fact, it was the life of the free desert communities. In the First Book of Samuel we see a distinct step forward; there is a king, and armies are brought into some kind of order; but still the culture is very low and crude. Yet two great strides forward were made at that time or in the years immediately following it. These were the introduction of iron, and the invention of alphabetic writing. The first of these is certainly, the latter probably, to be laid to the credit of the Philistines.

The history of the origin of the use of iron is in some respects problematical. Everything points to about 1000 B.C. as the extreme limit to which we can assign the use of iron objects found in Europe. The same is true of discoveries made in Asia Minor, the Levant coast, and the adjacent islands. But in a few individual cases in Egypt the use of this metal was somehow anticipated at a very early date—almost as early, indeed, as bronze—but never to such an extent as to become general. Whether certain persons discovered for themselves the art of smelting and working iron (which is really not more difficult than the corresponding operation applied to copper, and indeed is less recondite than the process of making

bronze by alloying two different metals) and died
without publishing their secret ; or whether, as is
more likely, the iron-bearing ores were not discovered
in sufficient quantity to make their working profitable
till the late date above given, cannot be certainly
asserted.

A passage in the Book of Samuel[1], obscure and
corrupt—in part indeed unintelligible—points clearly
enough, notwithstanding, to the conclusion that it
was the Philistines who introduced the use of iron
to the country which they occupied. No smith was
in Israel—the Philistines carefully retained the
monopoly of working in the new metal—and except
the king and the king's son no one was able to
procure an iron sword: all had to make shift with
ox-goads or other agricultural implements. The
passage asserts almost in as many words that the
Hebrews were still in the Bronze, the Philistines
already in the Iron Age. The break-up of the
Philistine domination removed the embargo on the
new metal, and when David was on the throne its use
became general. With the spread of iron, flint—
which, as we have already said, was still used as a
material for rough cutting implements—was quickly
discarded. The excavations reveal facts pointing to
the same conclusions.

It is interesting to note that the use of iron was at

[1] 1 Sam. xiii. 19–22.

first avoided in connexion with religious undertakings. The passage 1 Kings vi. 7 does not imply (as is commonly supposed) that the temple rose *in silence*: it means that its stones were not profaned by the touch of this new metal. (Compare Exod. xx. 25).

Even greater obscurity shrouds the origin of the alphabet in which were written such ancient fragments of Hebrew, Phoenician, and allied languages as have survived. This wonderful achievement is commonly ascribed to the Phoenicians, but without any grounds beyond ancient Greek tradition. That the Phoenicians, true to their function as merchants and middlemen, imparted a knowledge of alphabetical writing to the Greeks need not be questioned: but as knowledge grows it becomes increasingly difficult to believe that they were capable of the enormous analytic feat of devising an alphabet whereby the simple sounds of their language were written down. The far more cultured Babylonians and Assyrians, notwithstanding their extensive and varied literary activity, never even began to evolve an alphabet from their complex syllabaries. The Egyptians maintained all the cumbrous machinery of syllabic signs, determinatives and the rest until an alphabet of Greek origin was introduced and swamped them. How then could it be reserved for the Phoenicians to attain to what these great nations never could reach ?

The question is still open: but when the future

brings its solution it will probably be found that the
Philistines had a large share in developing this great
gift to mankind. They came from a country where
a form of script had been practised from remote
times, originally hieroglyphic, but, with the sound
practicality of the Cretans, early modified into a
linear character. There is considerable resemblance
between certain of these linear signs and the letters
of the so-called Phoenician alphabet, though this
must not blind us to the fact that there are also
many differences, and that so far attempts to correlate
the two systems of writing have not been very
successful. But not much can be expected one way
or another till the happy day comes when the Cretan
tablets have been deciphered.

It is true, no trace of pre-Exilic writing, in any
native language other than Semitic, has yet been
found in the mounds of the maritime lands of
Palestine. This is not to be wondered at—the
majority of documents would no doubt be written
on perishable materials; and exploration has so far
not exhausted the possibilities of any of the mounds,
even of those where excavations have been made.
Till some such discovery be made, the question of
the origin of alphabetic writing must remain a
matter of speculation. As the oldest relics of the
alphabet have been found on the Syrian coast and
among Semitic peoples in the lands immediately west

or east of it[1], it was presumably evolved somewhere
in that region; and assuming this, it is difficult to see
what people other than the Philistines were capable
of this great achievement.

CHAPTER V

THE HEBREW MONARCHY

THE Monarchy, once the Hebrew people had
attained to that stage of evolution, developed rapidly.
Saul was scarcely more than a glorified tribal sheikh,
ignorant, superstitious, coarse and boorish of tongue,
but while his health lasted a good leader and a good
fighter. Forty years afterwards a typical oriental
king was on the throne—wealthy, voluptuous, and
oppressive to his people. There could scarcely have
been a greater contrast than Saul and Solomon. The
disruption of the kingdom into its two elements—
never very firmly cemented together—produced little
change in the character of the Monarchy, either of
the north or the south. The lurid picture drawn by
Amos shews us the luxury and overbearing of the
wealthy classes which we find in every community
of the East.

[1] *I.e.* in Cyprus on the one hand and Moab on the other.

For the details of the history during this period, reference must be made to the familiar sources of information.   Our function is to trace briefly the development of culture.   The wars of David, foreign and civil, were hardly calculated to foster the arts of peace ; but his reign was marked by the extension of the two great auxiliaries to civilization whose introduction we noticed in the preceding chapter. Iron added countless new possibilities to life; and the simple alphabet rendered possible the beginning of a literature which was quite unattainable through the medium of the complex syllabaries that preceded it.   Whatever may be the date of the various compositions to be found in the Psalter, as we have it, the tradition that David was himself a poet is too constant and too definite to be lightly set aside. Solomon, too, was an author, whatever the origin of the books traditionally ascribed to him may be: 1 Kings iv. 31–33 credits him with collections of proverbs, poems, and speculations on natural history. This is the only hint at an interest in natural science as such that we find in ancient Hebrew history. A fascinating sentence, however, in this passage shews how imperfect our knowledge necessarily is: we would fain have heard something of the four totally forgotten sages, Ethan, Heman, Calcol, and Darda, whose wisdom was worthy of affording a scale by which to measure that of Solomon.

A certain stimulus was given to architecture and the allied arts by the building operations of Solomon; especially, no doubt, at Jerusalem itself. It was, however, necessary for him to send abroad for his chief artificers; the Hebrews themselves were incapable of erecting buildings desired to be 'exceeding magnifical.' The king frankly admits that 'there is not among us any that can skill to hew timber like unto the Zidonians.' Hiram, Solomon's ally, sent timber, and also sent (to superintend the work) a foreman builder, who happened to have the same name as himself, the son of a Phoenician father and a Hebrew mother.

Thus, the works built during Solomon's reign were carried out by Phoenicians, no doubt in the style which the Phoenicians had learnt from Egypt and from the remnant of Crete. There is not one stone of Solomon's Temple remaining on another, and it is hopeless to try to reconstruct it from the insufficient data given in the Book of Kings and in Josephus. Heroic attempts have been made to do so, but the results are at variance with each other and with any architectural style that would be probable at the time of the construction to such an extent, that no reliance can be placed upon them.

In the country towns we hear of fortifications being erected under Solomon's auspices. Remains of some of these, at Megiddo, Taanach, and Gezer, have been identified with a certain amount of probability. They display massive masonry, of fairly large and well squared stones, which, apparently for the first time in the country, are often drafted.

In the minor arts no special improvement or novel influence is to be detected. Pottery for instance remains a crude and feeble degradation of the Aegean style; it indeed becomes more and more coarse and debased as time goes on, and as copies are made from copies and not from the prototypes. There is a total absence of any evidence of even a desire for originality. The patterns with which vessels were ornamented in the late Canaanite period disappear altogether, and their place is occupied by plain painted lines and coarse mouldings. In the same way such jewelry as is to be found is either imported directly from Egypt or is obviously founded on contemporary Egyptian models.

But Solomon made further attempts at an advance in civilization. Seeing the profit his Phoenician neighbours made by their trading vessels, he determined to set up a fleet of merchantmen for himself. The Mediterranean, however, was already occupied by the Phoenician ships, and to have attempted to trespass on their preserves would, no doubt, have led to trouble. But at the head of the Red Sea he found an outlet for his energies, and he carried on a trade with the lands of the South, apparently with success. Even in this enterprise, however, he was compelled to employ Phoenician sailors (1 Kings ix. 27). The Hebrews were landsmen, and indeed had had no opportunities of practising the science of navigation. When Jehoshaphat attempted to revive this trade, his Red Sea fleet was wrecked ignominiously before it left its harbour at Ezion-Geber.

In many of the incidents narrated in the course of the history of the Kings we see strangely reflected unchanging Semitic psychological traits, an understanding of which is necessary to the comprehension of the narrative. Every modern Bedawy chief would sympathise with Hadad the Edomite[1], albeit his position was incomprehensible to the Egyptian king who had heaped favours upon him and even given him a royal Princess to wife. Everyone who has had traffic with orientals can understand how the irresistible impulse of hospitality, quite heedless of any possible inconvenience to the guest, compelled the old prophet of Bethel[2] to force the strange 'Man of God' to return with him, contrary to the express commands the latter had received.

But thanks to Muhammad, there has been one great change for the better. Drunkenness must have been a common vice: we read of the intoxication of Nabal, of Zimri, of Ben-Hadad:—even among women

---

[1] 1 Kings xi. 14.
[2] 1 Kings xiii. 11.

it was perhaps frequent though condemned, for Eli
thought that Hannah was under the influence of
wine[1]. The total eradication of this vice is one of
the strongest testimonies to the power of Islam.

No doubt the widening breach between the
northern and southern kingdoms served to retard
the course of civilization. The constant border wars,
rarely interrupted by alliances between individual
kings, and the perpetual atmosphere of anxiety these
must have caused, were quite sufficient to hinder
progress in the arts of peace. Only one city—Samaria
—was added by the Hebrews to the cities they
inherited from their Canaanite predecessors. Only
one king attempted to rival Solomon in the sump-
tuousness of his buildings: this was Ahab, who is said
to have built an ivory palace, but, like everything else
he did, this was no doubt under the influence of his
energetic Phoenician wife. Ahab himself is revealed
throughout his history as a despicable creature.
Ahab calls Elijah abusive names, but he meekly does
what the prophet tells him, and humbles himself
before him on every occasion; a word from Jezebel
was enough to make even Elijah flee to Horeb. Ahab
displays a feeble good nature toward Ben-Hadad even
after defeating him, with disastrous consequences to
his country and himself. When Naboth refuses to
sell his vineyard, the King of Israel can do nothing

[1] 1 Sam. i. 14.

more than go to bed in a fit of childish sulks; Jezebel
vindicates outraged majesty. In the final scene he
ingeniously manages that Jehoshaphat shall represent
him and be a target for assaults meant for himself:
he slinks about the battle in disguise till a chance
arrow finds him out. This is all we know about
Ahab, and it is a truly sandy foundation on which to
erect the extravagant eulogies showered upon him
by Renan and others.

Possibly Omri, and certainly Jeroboam II, and in
the southern kingdom Uzziah, were kings that distinguished themselves in more than mere fighting.
But there can hardly be any doubt that to the end
the civilization they affected remained exotic, pur-
chased in the great centres of culture around, and
obtained at the expense of the country at large. The
indignation of the rough rustic Amos is roused by
the sight of the 'notable men of the chief of the
nations' at Samaria languidly reclining on their ivory
couches, eating of the choice of the meat, drinking
wine by the bowlful, and tickling their ears with
music. All these things had to be paid for, and
Palestine, a country with no mineral resources, had
nothing but its agricultural produce to offer in ex-
change. Even the more wealthy of the common folk
could not venture to share in these delights, for whoso
made a display of expensive comforts attracted to
himself the unwelcome attention of the tax-gatherer.

Apart from military fortifications we know of but one piece of work undertaken for the public good during this period, and even that was military in essence, being intended to secure a supply of water to Jerusalem in case of siege. This is the Siloam tunnel, which carries water from the spring now known as the Virgin's Fountain to the Pool of Siloam, a tank once included by the city walls. It is a pathetically helpless piece of engineering. The labourers started from each end apparently without guidance, and penetrated in a course nearly twice as long as was needed, until by a miracle the two parties approximated near enough to hear each other's picks. An Egyptian engineer, or even the ancient Canaanite who carried out the tunnel at Gezer, would have taken a pride in cutting something better than this irregular and ill-finished passage, winding its random way beneath the foundations of the City of David.

CHAPTER VI

THE CAPTIVITIES AND AFTER

THESE luxurious and corrupt kingdoms were abruptly cut short. The Assyrian swooped down on the northern kingdom, and having carried its people away dispersed them in a number of new lands. Here, divided and with no possibility of a leader to keep alive their national traditions, they finally lost their individuality and became absorbed in the nations among whom they were planted. In their stead a mixed multitude from other sources was established in the lands of Samaria, who grafted on to their several ancestral beliefs the religion of 'the God of the land,' and who, maintaining their position through all the subsequent vicissitudes, still survive as that strange fossil of history, the tiny Samaritan community of Nablus.

The southern kingdom survived its northern neighbour for nearly 150 years ; but in time it shared the same fate, though in a modified degree. Their milder masters, the Babylonians, did not set themselves deliberately to break the spirit of their captives, as the Assyrians had done with complete success. They permitted them the exercise of their religion and the inspiration of such teachers as Ezekiel. Thus were the national instincts stimulated and the way prepared for the return from captivity.

During the absence of the captives there is very little to tell of the history of Palestine, and still less regarding its civilization. The Assyrian script, speech, and legal formularies were used by whatever garrison the King of Assyria left behind in the northern kingdom. A couple of tablets found at Gezer illustrated this. But the Assyrian civilization was purely exotic

and made no impression on the country as a whole.
No doubt the dregs of the Hebrew population were
left behind in both the north and the south.   From
these the conquerors had nothing either to fear or to
gain, and it was useful to keep the hewers of wood
and drawers of water to the tasks to which they were
accustomed.

A number of the Southern Hebrews escaped with
Jeremiah to Egypt.   The Aswân Aramaic papyri
have been supposed, but perhaps questionably, to be
records of this community of exiles.

Whatever Hebrew element may have remained in
the northern kingdom became absorbed into the
new settlers, who in part at least had adopted their
religion and so paved the way for union.   We therefore hear no more about them, except in so far as
their blood dilutes that of the Samaritan community.
The Southern Hebrews had no such temptation to
lose their separate existence.   They were pressed on
all sides ; by the remnant of the Philistines in the
west, the Bedawin in the east and south, the
Samaritans (as we may henceforth call them) in the
north ; and though in evil case, this pressure of
hostile aliens served to keep them faithful to their
national inheritance.   Being for the greater part
representatives of the tribe of Judah, the only important sept that survived, they adopted that name
as a designation, rather than the national name of

Hebrew which had included all the rest. It is now for the first time that we meet with 'Jews.' The use of this name should be avoided in speaking of the pre-exilic history. To call Moses the leader of the Jews, and to refer to David or Solomon as kings of the Jews, are anachronisms.

The Kingdom of Judah fell in 586 B.C. In 538 B.C. the first 'instalment' of the return, that led by Zerubbabel with the permission of Cyrus, made its way back and reinforced the harassed remnant that had remained in the country. The years following may be called the Persian period of the History of Palestine. From the point of view of culture, it was a time of transition. The beginning of the Hellenic domination in the realm of civilization, destined a few generations later to be complete, may now be traced in some of the objects that excavation has revealed. Zerubbabel and his fellow-leaders began a restoration of the temple and of the walls of Jerusalem. Naturally the Samaritans and the Bedawin, who looked on the land of milk and honey as their destined prey, endeavoured to hinder the work of restoration, but, so far at least as the temple was concerned, they could not prevent its completion. This took place in 516 B.C. About 60 years later Ezra brought back a further contingent of the captives, and the work of restoration of the city walls was begun by Nehemiah in 445. The book of the law was promulgated, the elaborate ritual reorganized, and the State of Jerusalem established, which endured until the destruction of the city by Titus in 70 A.D. It was, however, obliged to submit to Alexander the Great, who conquered Syria in 333 B.C., and to Ptolemy Soter, who took possession of the country in 320. In 314 Antigonus took Palestine, and thus began a contest between Egypt and Syria for the possession of the country which lasted spasmodically for over 100 years. In 175 B.C. Antiochus Epiphanes set himself to destroy the Jewish religion and to foster Hellenic ideas. He was met by the Maccabean revolt, which under the leadership of the heroic brothers, Judas, Jonathan and Simon, ultimately (in 142 B.C.) established Judaea as an independent theocratic state, whose visible ruler was the High Priest. This endured till 63 B.C. when Pompey captured the city. In 37 B.C., Herod with Roman aid, captured Jerusalem and became its king by favour of the Roman Republic.

Such, in barest outline, is the complicated history of this period. When we study the remains that have come down to us, we find that the leading impression they make is the rapid growth of Greek ideas in the country. The religion, art, and language of Greece influence the culture of Palestine with a force ever increasing as the years pass on. One of the most glorious monuments of the best period of

Attic art that has come down to us was found in Syrian soil—the so-called sarcophagus of Alexander, discovered in a tomb at Sidon; and it is not merely an isolated specimen, witnessing to the enterprise of some exceptionally enlightened Sidonian, for in the same necropolis were other sarcophagi, in design and execution inferior only to this supreme work of art. Trade with Greece is amply attested by fragments of figured vases, both red and black, which are found in strata of the period, and by terracotta statuettes. Small figures of Greek divinities shew that such were worshipped, if only by Greek merchants settled in the country. A very extensive trade was carried on in Rhodian wine; countless handles of the wine-amphorae, stamped with governors' or merchants' names, are to be found through the whole country. Every ship that landed these vessels at the harbour must have contributed its share to the process of Hellenization. Classical architecture was copied, though its principles were never clearly understood by the native architects, and thus we find such curious mixtures of style as on the so-called Tomb of Absalom at Jerusalem, which presents us with *Ionic* pillars, supporting a *Doric* frieze, and a cornice above that if anything is Egyptian in its analogies.

The infusion of Greek ideas was thus inevitable, and was not due to the influence of the Syrian or the Egyptian monarchs, who did what they could

to advance it. In fact the attempts, especially that
of Antiochus Epiphanes, to force on the complete
Hellenization of the Jews, defeated their own end,
as persecutions always do. The gradual spread of
a leaven is very difficult to check ; the pressure of
a tyrant provokes immediate opposition. In spite of
Hellenizing traitors in the camp of the Jewish Church
itself, who were ready to carry out the schemes of
the Syrian pagan, the Jews successfully resisted
force with force, and the little knot of those faithful
to tradition maintained themselves in Jerusalem and
in the district around.

On the other hand, though those living under the
shadow of the temple might conserve their traditions,
the country districts underwent many changes. The
most noteworthy of these was the change of script
and language. Some jar-handles, stamped with
potters' names, belonging to the very end of the
monarchy or the beginning of our present period,
still display what is known as the Old Hebrew script.
This is an alphabet identical (to all intents and
purposes) with the Phoenician. On the coins struck
at Jerusalem by the High Priests, after the successful
issue of the Maccabean wars, this script continues
in use, in a rather cursive style: while at the same
time we begin to find, in inscriptions of a less formal
kind, such as graffiti, a considerably modified form of
the alphabet which is the immediate parent of the

familiar square Hebrew character of printed books. This, during the first century A.D., ousted from common use the earlier form, which, however, still survives in the script of the Samaritan community.

The Hebrew language disappeared before the Aramaic tongue of the Edomites and other Eastern septs that still pressed in upon the country. But neither language could stand before Greek, which by the time of Our Lord had practically become the current tongue of the whole land. Coins bore Greek legends : inscriptions, both formal and scribbled, are for the greater part in Greek : in rock-cut tombs, the limestone boxes (containing the bones cleared from the graves to make way for fresh interments) often bear scratched on them the name of the owner of the bones, and even on those found around Jerusalem at least one-half of the names are in Greek letters. Though Our Lord's mother-tongue was Aramaic, the fact that such Aramaic words as from time to time He used are recorded *literatim,* suggests that the language He habitually employed in all but the most familiar intercourse, and when under strong emotion, was something different.

The painted tomb of Apollophanes found at Beit Jibrin—by tomb-plunderers, unfortunately—is a favourable example of the art affected in the country during this period. And here as at all other times it is exotic. The figures of animals and wreaths are the work of some provincial (Egyptian ?) artist, following Greek models, and using the Greek language. Nay, even the casual visitors to this tomb—such as the pair of lovers who scratched a quaint amatory dialogue on the jamb of the doorway—used the Greek tongue, as their graffiti shew.

CHAPTER VII

THE GROWTH OF THE RELIGIOUS CONSCIOUSNESS IN ISRAEL

PALESTINE was the scene of the historical events round which our Faith is crystallised ; herein lies the especial importance of the country ; and no view of its civilization would be complete unless an endeavour be made to trace the steps by which its unique position was attained. The subject, however, cannot be adequately treated in a single chapter of a small book, and in such limits very little novelty is possible. The statement often made in popular books that 'the Bible is the best guide to Palestine' is grotesque ; but it is emphatically true that a knowledge of Palestine, its customs and ways of thought, is indispensable to a proper understanding of the Bible.

In the present chapter we are to trace (so far as our limits permit) the development among the

Hebrews of an instinct that they had a mission to fulfil in the world : that for some reason which they themselves never fully realised they were the 'chosen people.'

We must recognise from the first that, as in all developments, fossils of earlier conditions were preserved even down to a late date. We are startled by such in both the historical and the legal divisions of the Pentateuch. Notable cases are the legend of the unions of 'the sons of God and the daughters of men' in the one[1], the strange magical water-ordeal for testing conjugal fidelity[2] in the other. It is necessary to study the subject *ab ovo*, so to speak, and to go back to the Bedawin from which in remote times Israel sprang, in order to account for all the details with which we meet.

The free life of the Bedawy is proverbial ; and yet there are probably few primitive races so limited in their outlook, mental and physical. Even his wanderings over the vast region which he inhabits are restricted—partly by the wide extent of sandy deserts incapable of supporting life, and partly by the hostility of rival tribes : the existence of most Bedawin is an eternal monotonous pilgrimage from watering-place to watering-place within a certain narrow limit of territory occupied by the tribe to

---

[1] Genesis vi. 1.
[2] Numbers v. 11.

which they belong. But the mental limitations of the Bedawy are even more rigid. The bare necessities of life are hard to come by, and must be strenuously fought for against nature and against his fellow-man ; and the fight practically absorbs all his energies and thoughts. A Muslim friend of the writer, who travelled to Medina on the first train of the Mecca railway, told how at the various stations on the way the wild Bedawin crowded round this marvel from the West that had disturbed the slumbers of their ancient land. But the wonders of the engine made not the smallest impression upon them. Their mental development was not sufficient to appreciate mechanical ingenuity. The only thing that aroused their enthusiasm was the plentiful store of *food* in the restaurant car. This fell within the narrow limits of their comprehension.

In the thirsty land, the spring of water and the spreading tree, or the rock that affords a grateful shade, are readily recognised as the gifts or even the actual manifestations of a divine power. These in-animate features of nature were the first messengers of God to man. The gloom of the valley or of the cavern first spoke of the Divine awe ; the cooling waters spoke of the Divine beneficence. There is, no doubt, an element of truth in the hackneyed gibe that man has made his god in his own image ; the deities of the earliest Semites (so far as we can discern their nature from the relics of these primitive beliefs that are embedded in all the later records) are clearly modelled on the Bedawy sheikh. As the sheikh is favourable to his own people, so is the tribal god : as the sheikh is hostile to all other clans, so is the tribal god. As the jurisdiction of the sheikh is strictly localised within the limits of the clan, and the area of land in which are situated the camping-places of the clan, so is the jurisdiction of the tribal god. As the sheikh's life consists of an endless succession of plundering raids, wherein he is alternately the offending or defending party, varied by indulgence in the most elementary pleasures of the senses, so does the life of the tribal deity, magnified in so far as his greater power gives larger opportunities. As a celibate sheikh is unimaginable, so must a female partner be found for the tribal god. To claim, as some have done, that the life of the desert favours the development of a monotheism, is the most crude absurdity : if a central government be inconceivable on earth, much less can it be imagined in the abode of the gods. Strange rocks, strange springs, strange groves of trees have each one its local *numen* to be propitiated in his own way ; even in comparatively late historic times we find that new-comers must learn 'the manner of the god of the land' when they would sojourn in his territory, and *per contra*, David must 'serve other gods' when he is driven into exile, and Naaman must provide himself with two mules' burden of the earth of Palestine when he would erect an altar to the God of Palestine in his Syrian home.

There was, besides, an elaborate demonology, of jinn, afrits, ghuls, and the like, which is developed most elaborately in Arab and Jewish folk-lore. These creations of the imagination probably take their rise in the terrors excited by noisome or dangerous animals. This is an interesting and fruitful, though an obscure and difficult subject; but for our present purpose it may be left on one side.

Such is the crude foundation of Semitic religion. Traces of it meet us everywhere, even to this day, as we have already seen (*ante*, p. 40). The natural conservatism which all people display in their religious rites and beliefs is nowhere more emphatically displayed than in the Semite. In fact, the more experience one has of the Semitic race, the greater becomes one's amazement at the organizing power of Muhammad and his immediate followers. That one man could drive his influence so deeply into that religiously unimpressionable people, is one of the most marvellous phenomena in the whole world's history. But even Muhammad was obliged to adopt into his system from earlier faiths that grievous burden, the Ramadan fast, and the toilsome pilgrimage to Mecca.

In studying the religious development of the Hebrews, two important points must be emphasised from the first. Israel was surrounded by the traditions of five great empires—Egypt, Assyria, Babylonia, the Hittites, and the Cretans. Directly or indirectly the Hebrews drew the whole of their secular arts, even the simplest, from one or other of these, as we have already seen: and in all material matters, peaceable or warlike, these empires were incomparably their superiors. And yet the polytheism of these imposing neighbours exercised no influence to speak of, upon the beliefs and ritual of the small and divided nation set in their midst. And the second point is like unto the first. Besides the great nations, Israel was surrounded by numbers of smaller tribes —Moab, Edom, Amalek, and the rest—their near kin in blood and language, and, in point of culture, very much on the same level with themselves. King Mesha of Moab, in his inscription, speaks of Israel and its king in much the same terms and probably much the same words as the latter would use of him. had an inscription giving us the other side of the story happily survived. And yet Israel, that unoriginal, semi-civilized people, who could not cut a tunnel straight through the rock of their metropolis, in the one realm of religion shot ahead of all their contemporaries and passed in the rapid course of a few centuries from polytheism (or perhaps more correctly polydaemonism) through henotheism to the uncompromising monotheism of the later prophets and psalmists. When we take into account first the environment, which was not only hostile to such a development, but even left no room or precedent for such a conception; and, secondly, the exaggerated conservatism of religion in the Semite, to which we have already referred : when also we take into account the natural unfitness for new ideas which Israel displayed in material affairs : we can but wonder in silence. Nothing like it has ever happened in the world. The miracles recorded in the Hebrew Scriptures may possibly in time be all accounted for, with the advance of natural or critical science: but each step taken in that direction only brings into greater prominence this central miracle of the Old Testament, which no amount of *soi-disant* Rationalism can explain away.

And the miracle was even greater than would appear from the above statement. For almost to the end of the monarchy the worship of the High Places was retained to its fullest extent. These were shrines, probably of vast antiquity in many cases, fitted out with the symbols of primitive Semitic worship, the standing stone, the sacred tree, and so on, where rites typifying the annual renewal of nature and allied ideas were carried on. It is no doubt unscientific to use depreciatory adjectives such as 'gross' or 'licentious' regarding these rites, as though they were wilfully indulged in for the special purpose of acting *contra bonos mores*: but we can scarcely doubt that they had such an influence on the character of those who took part in them as would make it yet more difficult for them to develop or to accept the prophets' definition of a Holy God.

Let us try in a few words to trace the steps by which the Hebrews were led along their unique path. It was the special privilege of this people that a succession of men was raised up from time to time who pointed out fresh steps of the road. Moses was the first of these. To his influence was due the formal adoption of the deity of Sinai as the God of the newly-founded nation, so that from the first the Hebrews worshipped a supreme God whose seat on earth was outside the territory which they occupied. This was very important. So long as a rigid local limitation hemmed in deities and their worshippers, progress was impossible: the work of Moses was the introduction of the conception of ex-territoriality. Suppliants like Elijah, when in dire straits, would make their way direct to the Mount of God: but in ordinary circumstances He could be enquired of in any of the shrines set up in His honour in the land of His adoption.

Of course the Mosaic system left the various local divinities where they were. These were propitiated and consulted freely. We may here mention Clermont-Ganneau's interesting suggestion that the strange and scarcely intelligible story of the apparition of the 'Captain of the Host (*sar-ṣebā*) of the Lord[1]' who appeared to Joshua on his entering the promised land, was really a vision of the *numen* of *Surṭabeh* (the great conical mountain that overlooks the Jordan valley at the point where the entrance must have taken place), thus encouraging and welcoming the new-comers. The Book of Judges is full of survivals and of indications that the people were still in an 'experimental' stage—their recurrent dallyings with the gods of the tribes round about, the sacred tree of Deborah, the idol made by Gideon, the sacrifice of Jephthah's daughter, the private oratory of Micah—all these are survivals of ancient rites and beliefs, not yet refined away.

To Samuel was due the second step. He seems to have grasped the idea that all these subordinate local deities were but manifestations of the one God of Israel. The school of prophets which he organized and directed no doubt helped to popularize this conception. Henceforth the High Places are shrines of Yahweh; and there is no reason to believe that any other deity was represented by the teraphim of David or the calves of Jeroboam: quite the contrary. At this point the polydaemonism of Israel becomes a

[1] Joshua v. 13.

henotheism. Chemosh and Milcom and other foreign
deities are actual entities, and notice must be taken
of them by a sojourner on foreign soil; but there is
one God only within the land of Palestine and He
only is to be there served. This, so stated, might
seem to be merely a return to the condition with
which we began: but there is this difference between
Yahweh and any of His rivals—He is still localised
outside His land, and He has now absorbed within
Himself all the petty deities of spring and forest and
mountain with which the fancies of the earliest
dwellers had peopled it.

Women as a rule are more tenacious of early
beliefs than men. This is especially true of Oriental
women, whose cramped existence makes them incapable from an early age of receiving new impressions.
Men, like David or Naaman, might under stress of
circumstances make a temporary or permanent
change in their religion without much searching of
heart; but a woman drafted into a royal harem is
likely to bring her own gods with her, and when the
husband is weak through senility like Solomon, or
constitutionally like Ahab, he is very apt to be
influenced by his partner to follow in her way. Thus
we find the disturbing element of foreign cult introduced by these two kings; but their influence was
only temporary and did not outlive them. When
Ahab's son had an accident, he did not trouble

himself about the Tyrian Baal, whom Ahab, under Jezebel's orders, had spent his energies in trying to impose upon his people: he sent off instead to an ancient oracle in the land of the Philistines. And similarly we hear nothing of Solomon's irregularities having any permanent influence after his death.

The third of the great religious leaders of the Hebrews was Asa, the king, inspired apparently by an obscure prophet named Azariah son of Oded. His work was ritual and moral, however, rather than doctrinal, and consisted in a purification of the rites and ceremonies at the shrines of the High Places. In him we see the awakening of a consciousness that the practices at these shrines were incompatible with true religion. Thus Asa set a standard of morality for all later time to which none of his predecessors had attained, and he is fully worthy of a place in the roll of the leaders of Hebrew thought.

The brilliant meteor-flash of Elijah, coming none knows whence, and going none knows whither, cannot be passed over altogether in silence, though the whole time of his labours was spent in leading the opposition to Ahab's religious innovations. It is, however, instructive to notice that there was never such strong opposition presented to any of the *legitimate* reforms of the national religion. It was as though attempts to lead the people away from the destined paths were fated to be specially resisted. Elijah is in this respect the forerunner of the Maccabees.

With Amos the herdman of Tekoa, who uttered his magnificent denunciation of the corruptions of Samaria in the reign of Jeroboam II, begins the long series of prophets who crowned the work of those who had prepared the way for them. We cannot give space to analyse their work in detail. Step by step an astonishing drama unfolds itself before us. Men come forward one by one, and speak now in impressive prose, now in poetry which for grandeur has never been surpassed on this earth, and one by one the calves, and the standing stones, and all the other ancient paraphernalia are thrown out as unclean things on the rubbish heap, and Israel realizes at last that the God whom for countless ages—back to the far off days of his nomad Bedawy life—he has ignorantly worshipped, He is the God of the whole earth. And this portent happens not among a reflective people like the Egyptians, or an artistic and philosophical people like the Greeks, or a practical nation like the Romans—but among the Hebrews, a people who were incapable of so much as making a clay waterpot without having a foreign model to copy —and even then made it clumsily !

It is not to be supposed that all the people, or even the majority, could rise to the heights of the prophetic inspiration. Both literature and the results of excavation forbid the idea. Down to a very late date small pottery models of cows are very common, which there can hardly be any doubt were popular images of the national God. The cult of the Queen

Fig. 5.   Terra-cotta Plaques 'pourtraying the Queen of Heaven.'
From examples found at Gezer.

of Heaven, denounced by Jeremiah (vii. 18, xliv. 13), is aptly illustrated by the plaques of terra-cotta[1] with

---

[1] These plaques are perhaps referred to by Jeremiah xliv. 18, in the phrase 'cakes to pourtray' the queen of heaven. The word translated 'cakes' is used only in the two passages relating to these objects.

figures of a female divinity in low relief stamped upon
them, found in numbers in every excavation ; such

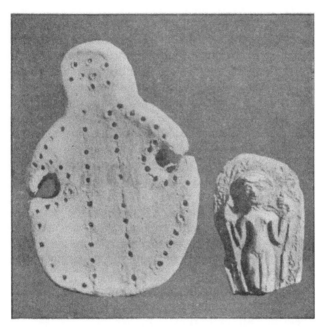

Fig. 6. TERRA-COTTA PLAQUES 'POURTRAYING THE QUEEN OF HEAVEN.'
Found at Gezer. (The left-hand example is highly conventional-
ised. It has also been explained as a board for some game, the
holes being meant for the reception of pegs. But they are too
small and too shallow for such a purpose.)

plaques were in use in Gezer even down to the time
of the Maccabees. The traditions set down by the
Yahvist and the Elohist reveal the simple anthropo-
morphisms of popular belief, that had their roots in
the primitive 'great chieftain' theory of deity. The
early chapters of Genesis shew that the notions of
cosmogony current in Palestine were at least founded
on the Babylonian stories of the beginnings of things.

But here again we meet with matter for wonder.
The wild tales of Marduk and Tiamat, of Gilgamesh
and the monstrous Ea-bani, of the gods gathering
like flies round the sacrifices, of all that welter of
weird imaginings—out of these unpromising materials
has been fashioned, with the most exquisite literary
taste and the most profound insight, an eternal
allegory of creative power, of sin, retribution, and
redemption, which a child can understand, yet whose
depths the wisest cannot fathom. And this has been
done by the Hebrews—a people who never during
their national existence made the smallest contri-
bution to material civilization!

To such people the prophets had to speak in terms
they could understand: indeed, they themselves had
their human limitations. In our own restless age,
when discoveries and inventions are antiquated almost
before they become generally known, we are beginning
to learn the changefulness of things. But in earlier
and quieter times this was not so. A Plantagenet

king or knight might endeavour to save his worthless
soul by making over a few acres of his land 'for ever'
to some shrine of St Thomas of Canterbury ; never
dreaming that the shrine was destined to fall in a
century or two under Puritan axes and hammers, and
the land, perhaps, to pass ultimately into the occupation of a worthy Nonconformist farmer, to whom
Becket is but a name in a half-forgotten school-book.
And likewise even the prophets of Israel clothed the
everlasting kernel they had discovered in a husk
belonging to their own time.   They or their auditors
were unable to conceive of the worship of their God
apart from the temple ; so they drew the gorgeous
dream-picture of a great central shrine for the whole
world, situated in Jerusalem.   It was reserved for a
Greater than they to break the husk, and to teach
that 'neither in this mountain nor in Jerusalem, shall
ye worship the Father......but in spirit and truth.'

But the husk, though broken, still conceals the
kernel for many, who have thus become obsessed with
an idea that the Jews are divinely fore-ordained to re-
people Palestine.   We can all warmly sympathise with
the *national* aspirations of a people which has behind
it a long record of oppression and persecution at
our Christian hands; but it is deplorable that theories
so materialistic should mingle with the *religion* of so
many Christian people.   From such a doctrine it is
but a step to the sheer lunacy of searching for the

lost ten tribes in this nation or that, or to the objectionable and presumptuous traffic in 'signs of the times.' It is not irrelevant, in a history of Palestinian civilization, to allude to this consequence of the formulae of the prophetic vision : because modern attempts to create an artificial 'fulfilment of prophecy,' whatever may be its ultimate outcome, cannot fail to modify the future history of the country in one way or another[1].

The elaborate legal restrictions to which the Jewish people submitted themselves after their return from the Babylonian captivity were designed to keep alive this great discovery. In the face of all the distracting influences to which they were exposed after they had re-established themselves in the Holy City, such restrictions were necessary. The persecutions of Antiochus saved the law from shipwreck on the rising tide of Hellenism ; and then the long mission of preparation entrusted to the chosen people was accomplished. 'For when the fulness of the time came, God sent forth His Son, born of a woman, born under the law, that He might redeem them which were under the law, that we might receive the adoption of sons.'

---

[1] A reviewer complained that I here 'go out of my way to denounce Zionism.' I have no such intention. These remarks are directed against a pseudo-Christian materialism that sees in the 'Return of the Jews' the first stage of a coming Millennium.

Thus the river, that rose in a bubbling spring in some Arabian oasis, flowed God-guided into the Ocean.

CHAPTER VIII

ROMAN AND BYZANTINE

THE Romans began to interfere in Palestinian politics in B.C. 63, when Pompey, in the course of his campaign against Tigranes, was called in to settle the dispute that had arisen between the brothers Aristobulus and Hyrcanus, successors of the valiant Maccabean leaders. The Jews however refusing to submit to the arbitration of a Gentile, Pompey laid siege to and captured Jerusalem, on which occasion he entered the temple and penetrated into the Most Holy Place. From this time onward the native kings ruled under Roman suzerainty. In the turmoil caused by a Parthian raid on the country, in B.C. 40, the Edomite (Idumaean) Herod managed to lay his hand on the governorship, and, having with Roman aid captured Jerusalem, he established himself as king in 37 B.C., of course by the consent and under the suzerainty of the Roman republic.

Herod seems to have set himself to imitate the traditional glories of Solomon. As Solomon built the temple and a fine palace, so did Herod. Indeed he improved upon the example of his prototype, for besides these buildings he erected a number of others designed to impress and to please the people. He built, for example, an amphitheatre at Jerusalem, the very site of which is now, however, unknown. So far as we can tell anything of the Herodian buildings at Jerusalem, they seem to have been entirely in Roman style, and probably were designed by Roman architects. Other cities, notably Samaria, were similarly enriched. The foundations of a gigantic temple on the summit of the mound of that city have been discovered in the course of the excavations conducted by Dr Reisner; and a second temple, a hippodrome, and a street of columns have always been conspicuous attractions to visitors to this site.

Herod died B.C. 4, and his kingdom was divided among various members of his family. This division made it easy for the Roman authority to usurp to itself all the real power, as is obvious throughout the narrative of the gospels. But the tension at last reached breaking point: the Jews revolted; and in 70 A.D. they were crushed by the terrible siege and the fall of Jerusalem.

The culture of this hundred and thirty years, between the siege of Pompey and that of Titus, has been very little illustrated by recent exploration. None of the sites excavated, with the exception of Samaria, have yielded any remains of importance belonging to this time. A few rock-cut tombs, the base of one of Herod's towers, the foundations of the temple enclosure, and some odds and ends, are all that remain within the City of Jerusalem of the activity of the great builder. Outside, the immense reservoirs between Jerusalem and Hebron probably, and the aqueducts by which water is carried thence to the former city certainly, were made under Roman superintendence about this time. From an old wives' tale that the pleasant valley where these reservoirs are situated was the scene of the Song of Songs, they are popularly called Solomon's Pools : the name is not altogether inappropriate if they be actually the work of the Edomite Solomon.

An important change was now taking place throughout the country. From the beginning people had lived huddled together in walled cities. But just about this time we find the walled cities are being deserted, and people are settling instead in wall-less villages. This is an eloquent testimony to the advantage for the country of the *Pax Romana*. It can hardly be an accident that the occupation of every walled city which has been as yet excavated in Palestine, with the possible exception of Samaria[1],

---

[1] Some Arab and Crusader work was found at Tell es-Safi, but there is a gap between this and older remains into which a ruined village of the Roman period, at the base of the mound, fits neatly. This apparent exception therefore accords with the rule.

ends just about the middle of the first century B.C.:
and that it is to this date that the earliest of the
numerous small ruins which dot the fields of the whole
country are to be assigned, if we may judge from the
sherds of pottery strewn on their surface.

The reason is very simple. The early cities were
set on hill-tops, a circumstance which, if it had the
disadvantage that they could not be hid, had the
important compensation that they could not be
attacked without difficulty, and could not be commanded from overlooking heights. While every
man's hand was against his neighbour, a hill-top city
surrounded by a high wall was the form which the
dwellings of the community assumed, of absolute
necessity. But the dwellers in the city had to pay
dear for the comparative security that this situation
gave them. The toilsome daily climb, the difficulty
of procuring water, the close and crowded existence,
the necessary remoteness from their crops in the
valleys—which an enemy might destroy before they
had time to come down to defend them—all these
drawbacks to city life must have been a constant
vexation. When we add that in the wars and dis-
turbances of the last five centuries B.C. the sedentary
population must have suffered considerable loss, so
that they were barely able to repair their walls if
broken down, or to defend them if repaired; we can
scarcely wonder that a time of peace was marked by

an exodus from these inconvenient towns. Little villages sprang up everywhere, situated in the very middle of the cultivated fields, and close to springs. These villages were often built of the materials of the old cities, and often bore the names of the old

Fig. 7.   Ruin of a Byzantine Village.

This ruin bears the name of the Biblical Tekoa, but as there is no trace of earlier occupation it cannot be on its exact site.

sites. This is the explanation of the anomaly which meets us over and over again when we try to study Bible Geography. We deduce from Biblical references

7—2

the probable district in which to find the site of a
certain town. We examine the map of the district,
and there we find a modern Arabic name almost
exactly resembling the old Hebrew name : and we
visit the site, confidently expecting to have the
pleasure of strolling over a great mound of accumulated *débris* and of wondering what may lie hidden
under our feet—but find when we reach the spot the
meagre remains of some wretched little Roman or
Byzantine village, with outcrops of rock in and
around it, shewing that no earlier remains can lie
beneath the surface. There are not merely five or
six, but dozens—it is hardly an exaggeration to say
hundreds—of such cases scattered in every corner of
Palestine and Syria. It cannot be said too strongly
that the identification of any Biblical site, based on
similarity of name alone, even if the locality be in a
suitable place, must never be allowed to pass un-
questioned. A personal examination of the ruins by
someone who has acquired a knowledge of the pottery
styles[1], and who can thus assign the limits of date

---

[1] Of the importance of potsherds in helping to the identification
of ancient sites one example may be given. The writer thinks he
may venture to claim to have settled the long-fought dispute concerning the site of Capernaum, in favour of *Talhum* as against the rival
sites, 'Oreimeh* and *Khan Minyeh*. The scanty fragments of pottery
at Talhum are of just the right date, those of 'Oreimeh are far too
early, and those of Khan Minyeh too late. It follows that Talhum
is the correct site.

of the occupation, is absolutely indispensable. It
will be found *in the majority of cases* that the
identifications put forward with confidence by
Robinson and other even more recent topographers,
fail when tested by this criterion. The old name
has been transferred, with the building materials.
In a generation the old site is forgotten: in a century
or two no one knows that there was a city there at
all, and some new and trivial name may be given to
the mound that covers it. Hence arises a two-fold
perplexity for the student of Historical Geography:
the number of large and important mounds bearing
names of no significance ; and the number of insignificant sites bearing names of the foremost importance.

The abortive rising of Simon Bar-Cochba, in
132–5 A.D. had no effect but that of making even
more determined the attempts of the Emperors to
Romanize Palestine. Hadrian re-founded Jerusalem
as a pagan city, with a Temple of Jupiter on the site
of the Jewish Temple, and (it is alleged) a Temple of
Venus on the site of the Holy Sepulchre; forbade
the Jews even to come within sight of the city ; and
attempted to break with all tradition by renaming
it Aelia Capitolina. This name, however, did not
survive long, unlike Sebaste, the name which Herod
the Great gave to Samaria in honour of Augustus[1],

[1] A name however ignored, perhaps with intention, by New
Testament writers, *e.g.* St Luke (Acts viii. 5).

and Flavia Neapolis, the new name of Shechem, given it after its conquest by Vespasian in 67 A.D. These names, as Sebusteh and Nablus respectively, still survive as the current names of these towns. Banias (= Paneas), Kuloniyeh (= Colonia), Trablus (= Tripolis), Fundakumiyeh (= Pentecomias), are other examples of the survival of exotic place-names in modern Arab Palestine, but such are uncommon.

Apart from roads, aqueducts, and other military or semi-military works, there are however no very conspicuous traces of Roman civilization in the country. The language remained Greek, and in this language are written by far the greater proportion of the inscriptions of this period that the country has yielded : comparatively few Roman inscriptions, if we except milestones, have come to light, and even these often bear inscriptions wholly or partly in Greek.

The Jews, driven thus from their capital at Jerusalem, found a resting place in Tiberias, a city that had been founded by Herod Antipas and so named in honour of the Emperor Tiberius. The community of Jews which thus centred in a city, previously avoided as heathen and unclean, must have had a curious internal history, of which not very much is known. Their literary monument is the so-called 'Jerusalem Talmud'; their tangible monuments are those very remarkable buildings the

Synagogues of Galilee, which still survive, though in
a sad state of dilapidation, from the beginning of the
third century A.D. These buildings throw unexpected
side-lights on the Judaism of their time. They are
rectangular, the doorways, with one exception, facing

Fig. 8. FAÇADE OF THE RUINED SYNAGOGUE AT MEIRON.

south. Within, a central space is marked off by
pillars along three sides of the building ; behind the
pillars runs an aisle. But the remarkable point
about the Synagogues is their sculpture. Not only

are classical mouldings and ornament the basis of
the rich decoration which all these buildings bear,
but representations of living creatures, lions, eagles,
and the like are freely introduced, and even human
figures.   Nay, even such heathenish figures as genii
with swags and garlands, and centaurs, are occasionally to be found ; notably in the highly ornate but
much ruined Synagogue at Kerazeh (Chorazin).

Meanwhile, Christianity was spreading throughout
Europe, and those who submitted to its sway were
beginning to feel the desire to see its birthplace for
themselves.

At the head of the endless march of pilgrims
comes the Empress Helena (326 A.D.) who zealously
set herself to identify and to commemorate the sacred
scenes on which her Faith was founded.   The Church
of the Nativity at Bethlehem, the Holy Sepulchre at
Jerusalem, and the foundations of the great Church
discovered in the year 1911 on the Mount of Olives,
are monuments of Helena's Christian enthusiasm.
It matters not a whit whether Helena was right or
wrong in her selection of the sites.   So far as it was
humanly possible, she built worthy memorials of the
great events she desired to commemorate, which
through all the subsequent changes, and despite all
the petty squabbles of rival sects, have been hallowed
by the continuous veneration of 1600 years.   Right
or wrong, that is as near as we shall ever get to such

a site as the Holy Sepulchre.   It is deplorable that
the Muslims should be obliged to guard Christians
from fellow-Christians in this Church : it is deplorable that such scenes as the ceremony of the Holy
Fire should disgrace it : but it is nothing but fatuity
to protest against these blemishes by exalting an
insignificant third-century rock-tomb into the tomb
of Joseph of Arimathea, by wasting good building-
land in laying out an imaginary restoration of Joseph's
garden, and by squandering hundreds of pounds
(which would have been so welcome for scientific
exploration !) on acquiring and maintaining the
resulting outrage on common sense.   If the shrine
of Helena inspires in some overstrung natures an
ecstasy of devotion dangerously bordering on hysteria,
the cult of the so-called 'Gordon's tomb' is mere
sentimentalism, without an atom of historical actu-
ality behind it.

A few years after Helena—in 333 A.D.—came a
nameless wanderer from Bordeaux, who worshipped
and departed to his home, where he wrote an
itinerary, all too short, of his travels.   Some random
details of Jerusalem topography which he vouchsafes
us—apparently chance recollections that happened
to recur to him when writing out his notes—are of
immense value, so far as they go.   Meagre though
it be, the Itinerary of the Bordeaux Pilgrim has
the distinction of being the first of the long series

of books written about Palestine from personal observation.

On the partition of the empire, in 394 A.D., Palestine naturally formed a part of the heritage of the East. It was by then practically completely Christian. All the tombs from that period which have been opened bear Christian devices or contain Christian relics. Churches and monasteries spread over the country, especially under the care of Justinian I, who carried out many important buildings —such as the Church of St Mary at Jerusalem, now (in a mutilated form) the Mosque *el-Aksa*.

Except for the sanguinary raid of Chosroes, King of Persia, in 616, life in the country during the Byzantine period seems to have been quiet enough. The multiplication of small villages without formal defences went on unchecked, and this in itself is an indication that the people on the whole lived in as much security as could be expected. Mosaic pavements of great richness, not only in Jerusalem but even in occasional village church sites, testify to an appreciation for art. The churches, though small, were often richly sculptured, and such fragments as remain are of great interest. No excavations have been formally carried out in any Byzantine sites, so that but little can be said about the life of the people; it was probably not unlike that which we see mirrored in one of the modern villages, such as

Jifna, Beit Jala, or Bethlehem, which have succeeded
in holding fast to the Christian faith that they trace
back to Byzantine Palestine.   Perhaps, like the
Plantagenets mentioned in the previous chapter, the
people thought that the clock of time would surely
now stand still—

But Arabia lies in the background, and Arabia
was full to overflowing : and through Arabia one
was journeying to and fro, driving camels, who was
soon to drive half the world.

CHAPTER IX

MUSLIM AND CRUSADER

Of Muhammad, let it suffice here to say that he
was born about 570 or 571; that about the age of
forty he began to feel a stirring of revolt within him
against the gods of his fathers; and that he devoted
the rest of his life to the development and the pro-
mulgation of the religion he proposed to substitute.
His models were now Judaism and now Christianity,
though he wofully misunderstood the historical basis
as well as the spiritual essence of both systems; and
he tempered them with his own spirit and with the
peculiar mental standpoints of his people, so that
he gave the product an individuality all its own

Slowly but surely, though opposed in a hundred ways, the movement spread, until for the first time in the countless ages of the past practically the whole of the peninsula realised that it was of one kin, as it was of one speech. The barriers burst, and Arabia, bound together by a common faith as it had never been bound before, poured forth on the fat lands to the north and west with a sheer dead weight that none could resist. The Byzantine empire crumbled away like straw before them. In 634 'Omar, the second successor of Muhammad, defeated its hosts at the battle of the Yarmuk, and shortly afterwards he captured Damascus and Jerusalem. Henceforth, save for the interlude described in this chapter, Palestine was a Muslim country. And Muhammad had not been in his grave a hundred years before Islam had spread from Baghdad to Spain.

The new rulers began well. 'Omar set an example of tolerance to his new Christian subjects that was rare in those early days, and is by no means universal even in our own enlightened times. The Christians were permitted to retain the Holy Sepulchre Church and to continue their worship without interference. But naturally they could not expect to have it all their own way as heretofore: there were curtailments of their liberty here and there which they deeply resented, but could not overcome, and as time went on these tended to increase.

The rigid puritanism of the Muhammadan system, in matters of art, did not make for any very high level of culture. The representation of living creatures was *tabu* to an extent that had never been equalled before. Geometrical ornament was the most that was allowed; and this, founded on Byzantine models, developed wondrously, till it reached a height of subtlety equalled only by the highest attainments of the Celtic artists.

For 'Abd el-Melek, the fifth from 'Omar, was reserved the honour of erecting a permanent building over the Holy Rock of the Temple site. This rock is the summit of the so-called Moriah, the Temple hill, and being the probable site of the altar of burnt sacrifice was sacred to the dispersed of Israel, in despite of whom the Christians during their time of domination had permitted it to become defiled with rubbish and filth. 'Omar cleansed it—for strange legends hallowed the Holy Rock in Muslim eyes as well—and, it appears, erected a temporary structure over it to preserve it from further profanation. For this structure 'Abd el-Melek substituted the far-famed Dome of the Rock, often inaccurately called the Mosque of 'Omar. The outlines of the exterior of this building are unpleasing, and even its gorgeous incrustation of blue tiles cannot altogether redeem its stiffness; but when we cross the threshold all is changed, and we are bewildered by a riot of beauty which no pen can adequately describe, and to which, perhaps, no pencil can do justice.   As we examine in turn the mosaics, the coloured windows, the split and polished marble slabs, the painted decoration, we are every moment confronted by some new flash of artistic inspiration that drives from our minds what we have been looking at the moment before.   Deplorable attempts at restoration and renovation—and even alteration—have been made in these days, when Arab art is but the pale ghost of its glorious youth. These are offences that diminish the effect the building would otherwise make : a yet greater offence is the persecution the visitor invariably suffers from the grovelling bakhshish-hunting custodians who never leave him for an instant alone.   Notwithstanding, there are surely few buildings in the world that make a deeper impression on the mind than does the Dome of the Rock.

And yet, though the Dome of the Rock reveals the strength of Arab art in those early days, it reveals its weakness too.   The canker of shoddiness, which has by now eaten it through and through, is already at work.   Thus, the pillars of the colonnade which surrounds the Rock were not specially made or designed for the building, but pillaged from any other structures that happened to possess them.   And so in this part of the Dome of the Rock we have a heterogeneous assembly of Corinthian and Byzantine pillars, which not being of uniform length are brought to a standard height by blocks, large or small as may be required, set on the tops of the capitals. These blocks do not improve the architectural effect of the building. In fact the art of the Arabs was always decorative rather than constructional. Their architecture depended almost entirely on its applied ornament for the effect it produced.

The first enthusiasm of unity soon wore off. Sects began to multiply. Unregenerate human nature began once more to assert itself, and the comparative quiet which had made the Dome of the Rock possible, gave place to a wild *Walpurgisnacht* of envy, hatred, and malice, which lasted for 300 years. Omayyades and 'Abbasides, Carmathians and Ikhshidides, Fatimites and Seljuks pass in turn before us; and though Arab literature attained to an important place during these troubled times, it is easy to understand that the endless quarrels and fighting between these rival clans made any advance in art and civilization impossible.

To re-tell the dreary story of those distracted centuries is not our purpose here. The climax was perhaps reached in the saturnalia inaugurated by the accession of the Fatimite caliph Hakim, in 996 A.D. The portent of a madman in absolute power was once more seen in this imperfect world of ours, with a completeness to be matched only in Rome under the

Caesars. But Caligula and Nero, a thousand years after they had gone to their own place, were on the earth as though they had never been; whereas to this hour the religion of the brave yet kindly Druzes of Lebanon is founded on the ravings of this maniac.

As might be expected, it was not long before the tolerance extended at first to the Christians gave place to persecution. They began to suffer, in like manner as they had made the Jews suffer in the day of their power. Their churches were desecrated, if not actually destroyed, as was the Holy Sepulchre by the Caliph Hakim; and they themselves were compelled to submit to many indignities. Pilgrims especially were subject to extortion and abuse of every kind. The spectacle of the troubles to which they were exposed set Europe on fire with a holy ardour to rescue the shrines of the Faith out of the hands of the infidel. (The romantic figure of Peter the Hermit has, alas, been expunged from the picture by modern historical criticism.)

Thus began the Crusades, the most far-reaching movement of the Middle Ages. A lifetime would scarcely be sufficient to trace out the causes that led to them, the complex history of the enterprises themselves, and their manifold influence on European politics, art, and literature. The first outburst of the movement strangely resembled the first outburst of Islam itself. As Islam united the scattered tribes of

Arabia, so did the Crusader zeal unite the warring nations of Europe into one irresistible whole ; and as Islam found nothing to oppose it but the moribund Byzantine empire, so the Crusaders found Islam torn in pieces and ready to perish from internal dissensions.

Though the waste of life was enormous in the first march on Jerusalem, Godfrey of Boulogne, destined to be the first of the Latin kings of Jerusalem, led his victorious army into the Holy City on the 15th July, 1099. And so began the century wherein once again West contended with East for Palestine. But Godfrey enjoyed his well-earned reign a year only. On his tomb—standing till the beginning of the last century, when it was destroyed in jealousy by a rival sect— was engraved the famous inscription :—

HIC IACET INCLITVS GODOFREDVS DE BOVILLON QVI
TOTAM ISTAM TERRAM ACQVISIVIT CVLTVI
CHRISTIANO CVIVS ANIMA REGNET IN CHRISTO[1].

Acquisiuit—in this well-chosen verb lies the condemnation of the Crusaders, which all unwitting the author of this inscription wrote. For once, Christianity fought Islam with its own weapon, and met the inevitable failure destined for them that take the sword.

[1] There are slight differences, chiefly in spelling, in the renderings of different copyists. The above is the version given by Henri de Beauveau in his *Relation journalière du voyage du Levant*, 1604.

MONS CALVARIVS

Fig. 9. The Tombs of Kings Godfrey and Baldwin I.

F is the tomb of Godfrey, E of Baldwin I. They are shewn below to a larger scale. G in the foreground is the Stone of Unction. In the background is the chapel of Mount Calvary, and to the left the entrance to the ambulatory behind the apse of the church. The tombs are now completely destroyed, and practically everything to be seen in the illustration has been re-modelled.

It is perhaps the saddest of all histories. As the sun rises hot and bright on a summer morning, so burns the glowing enthusiasm over Europe, and so shine the splendid first leaders of the advancing army. But clouds begin to gather soon, as jealousies arise within the newly-planted colony, and as the diseases with which warm climates punish ignorance and carelessness and indulgence break out among them: even the taint of leprosy spares not the throne itself. And the clouds darken to a deeper black as the day advances, for we hear yet darker tales of intrigues, and poisonings, and assassinations, and of disunion and unpreparedness in the face of Islam step by step retrieving its lost ground. Then comes the thunderburst of Hattin, and the Latin kingdom falls before the great leader, Salah ed-Din. And a chill night wind bears to our ears across the centuries the sound of the wailing of little children, as the sun sets in an angry, cruel red—fit emblem of the horrors unspeakable of the Children's Crusade of 1212 A.D.

The remarkably rapid degeneration, in both physical and moral well-being, which the Crusaders began to display almost immediately after establishing themselves in the goal of their desires, is probably to be explained in one word—malaria. If the Children of Israel were assisted in their invasion by 'hornets,' literal or metaphorical, the *Anopheles* mosquito is equally effective as a bulwark for the defenders against rash intruders. The mosquito always scents out a new-comer into its sphere of influence. Two people, one a stranger, the other a six months' resident, may sleep together in a room or tent; in the morning the first will be stung all over, the second will have been left untouched. Very likely every man in the army of the Crusaders was inoculated with malaria before he had been forty-eight hours within the borders where the disease was and is endemic. The demoralising effect of malaria on both mind and body is one of its most serious features; and when we think of the utter ignorance of medical or sanitary science that prevailed in the twelfth century—when we picture these men carrying habits of life suited to their temperate lands into the blasting siroccos of Palestine, we cease to wonder at the fate of the Latin kingdom.

The Crusader stock gradually died out; its last traceable descendants appear to have been hopelessly degenerate half-breeds. This is a point worth remembering, for there seems to be an idea current that the (alleged) beauty of the modern natives of Bethlehem is due to an infusion of Crusader blood. There is no necessity to seek a cause so remote. Bethlehem, thanks to its trade in mother-of-pearl, is a fairly wealthy village, and good feeding is quite sufficient to account for any superiority the inhabitants can claim over their less favoured neighbours.

Acquisiuit is not written only on Godfrey's shattered tomb. It is written large over the face of the land as well, and the letters with which it is spelt are the castles, still huge and imposing even in their gaunt ruin. It is written in the churches—some turned to mosques; some guarded against desecration by the devotion of recently established monasteries; some standing derelict and dilapidated in the open fields and valleys, and vanishing piecemeal before the builder who finds in them stone ready cut for his use. It is written in the hearts of the Arabs, who to this day tell of the great deeds their forebears did, when they slaughtered the Christians; and who teach to their children a deathless hatred of those who once *totam istam terram acquisiuerunt cultui Christiano.*

CHAPTER X

TILL YESTERDAY

THE Latin kingdom fell in 1187, but the ebbing wavelets of Crusader enthusiasm continued to beat on the shore of Palestine till 1248. A few coast towns were obstinately held by the Europeans—which, however, dropped from their hands one by one till at last Acre only was left. This resisted till

1291, and then the chapter of Frankish occupation was closed.

Once more Palestine and Syria became a prey to warring Asiatic tribes. Salah ed-Din, becoming master of Egypt soon after his victory at Hattin, united Palestine to the throne of that country. For rather more than 300 years it remained in the hands of the Egyptian sultans, though invaded and plundered from time to time by the Kharezmians from Central Asia and by the Mongols. So matters lasted till 1516, when war broke out between the Turks and the Egyptians. The former were victorious, and Palestine became thenceforward a Turkish province.

If the nation be happy that has no history, then Palestine for the next three centuries was truly favoured. A better illustration of the foolishness of this stupid proverb could not be found. The people of Palestine had no history—no relations with the great world around except through the intermediation of the Turkish tax-gatherer—no distractions or interests or resources or employments—nothing in short to occupy them save the ancient and unprofitable pastime of quarrelling among themselves. As time went on, Turkish rule became more and more nominal; so long as taxes were duly paid they might quarrel as they liked—indeed, is not *divide et impera* an ancient principle of sovereignty?

So the old divisions of Kais and Yaman, of North Arabia and South, transplanted among the sedentary fellah populations from their nomad ancestors, sundered neighbouring villages in an unending hostility that is but superficially healed even now. The tribal sheikhs practically directed all the affairs of the people : save that houses were substituted for tents, and that the Turkish master was ever in the background, the bad old traditions of Arabian desert life were perpetuated unchanged.

A few individuals stand out more conspicuous than their fellows in this long dull time of pointless turmoil. Such was the Druze prince Fakhr ed-Din, whose alliance with and sojourn among the Venetians inspired him with an unusual taste for European art; which he made a pathetic attempt to cultivate on the uncongenial soil of his native land. Such, for other reasons, was Ahmed the Butcher, who at the end of the eighteenth century established himself in a practically independent kingdom centring at Acre, and extending over all Northern and Central Palestine—a tyrant who for sheer loathsome savagery can scarcely be matched, even in the records of the kings of Assyria. Such, too, was the picturesque freebooter 'Akili Agha. But these are merely names that stand out the more conspicuously because they are set in a dead level of monotony.

From the incidents preserved to us by the pilgrims

and travellers of this time, who have left us records of their adventures, we see something of the social life of the country. Some of the more important of these are named in the bibliography at the end of this book. We must never forget, however, in using such authorities, that they were perforce superficial observers. A residence even of two or three years is not enough to give an insight into the inner heart of a community so complex and so foreign ; how then can we trust the judgment of a traveller scampering through the country, to whom every experience was a complete novelty, and every native a potential assassin ?

The capture of Jaffa and the Siege of Acre, by Napoleon I, in 1799, and the subsequent episode of the seizure of the country by the Egyptian rulers Muhammad Ali and Ibrahim Pasha, were the beginning of the end of this unsatisfactory condition of matters. The Turks, so soon as they had re-asserted their sovereignty after the Egyptian interlude, began a series of reforms, calculated to put down once for all the old sheikh government which had made life and property everywhere unsafe, and had made travel between the tribal territories difficult, if not impossible. The warring elements were brought together under at least a veneer of unity. Kais and Yaman were compelled to lay down their arms. Improved facilities of communication were established, and the

country once more entered into relations with Europe.
Compared with the intolerable excesses of such
creatures as Ahmed the Butcher, the rule even of the
worst of the Sultans was not too tyrannical. Under
Turkish rule Palestine might have become a prosperous
and happy country, but for the three inevitable con-
comitants of the government of that empire—the
growing burden of excessive taxation ; the corruption
of the local government officials ; and the necessary
ex-territorial privileges of foreigners, which put it in
the power of the unscrupulous to exploit the country
for their own selfish purposes.

Palestine, in short, has been a land of turmoil
from the early days of the Arab invasion : and that
in its manifold disorders there could be any advance
in civilization is unthinkable. The energy and skill
that gave to the land the Dome of the Rock and the
Mosque of the Omayyades in Damascus soon dwindled
away, and the decline was never checked. The
Crusaders were men of action rather than men of
learning, and they had not the time, even if they had
had the will, to foster art or civilization in the country.
After they left, matters went steadily from bad to
worse. To-day, even after the century of comparative
peace which has elapsed, there seems to be scarcely
the smallest comprehension of art in the Arab mind.
The wretched daubs with which the Jerusalem Mosque
was decorated, in preparation for the visit of the

German Emperor in 1898, are mournful witness to the fall from the high level on which was produced the Dome of the Rock.

In other directions civilization is at a standstill. The custom of holding village lands in common, distributed annually among the ploughmen by lot, is fatal to agricultural improvement. Old clumsy methods are followed, and probably not half the harvest is gathered that might be obtained. Of course there was, till yesterday, a further reason for this lack of enterprise ; if the grounds of a village brought forth plentifully, under the old *régime*, the tax-gatherer would put an impost on the village far exceeding a due or just proportion. There was thus every discouragement offered to industry, and as Palestine must ultimately depend almost exclusively on its produce, the country at large suffered with the farmers. A total lack of public spirit or of patriotism was another prime cause of the want of progress. 'Every man for himself' was the ruling principle of the community.

On the other hand, public works of great importance have been carried out, in the face of many difficulties, within the last 25 years : such are the networks of roads which now intersect the country : the railways to Damascus, Jerusalem, and the Hijaz : the water-supply of Jerusalem : the establishment of settled towns at Beersheba, 'Amman, Jerash, etc.,

which (though the important ancient ruins at these
places have been lamentably pulled about to supply
materials for the new buildings) serve the useful
purpose of outpost stations on the border of the
territory of the nomads. All these are signs of
progress. It is also true that various industries
flourished, in spite of Government interference. The
silk-weaving trade of Lebanon, the orange business
at Jaffa, the soap factories at Nablus, these and others
may be mentioned as goodly sources of income.

The native civilization, such as it is, is a painful
illustration of the evils of what may be called
unredeemed practicality. Listen to the conversation
of two casual wayfarers ; it is *always* about money,
generally small sums, reckoned in *beshliks* (sixpences).
A has sold a thing for so much—*B* has bought something else for so much—*C* has engaged himself as
cook, and gets so much wages—*D* owes so much to *E*
—*F* chiselled so much out of *G*—*H* is going to marry
K's daughter, and is paying so much for his bride—
these are the staple subjects of conversation. The
sole topic of interest is this single weariful subject of
the relations of life reduced to one uniform standard
of petty cash. A friend of the writer overheard
a youth telling his companion that if he had a magic
wishing-cap, he would desire a palace built of gold
and silver bricks, with a delicious soft divan on which
he would lie at his ease and do nothing all day but

smoke a water-pipe. The youth was a type. Riches, to gain the power of making display and the privilege of luxurious vacuous idleness—that is the aspiration of the town-bred Arab.

In such a community, the interests that to a western seem almost essential to the happiness of life are scarcely thought of. Literature is neglected; historical monuments are allowed to fall into ruin, to be taken down for building material, to be destroyed in one way or another, and no one cares; as for art, except delicate work turned out by the silversmiths and carpenters of Damascus, which can be highly praised, there is practically none. Nowhere can the mental blight caused by the love of money be more profitably studied.

One of the immediate consequences of the pacification of the country under Turkish rule has been the colonization of parts of the country by various communities of Europeans and Americans, and also the settlements of numerous individuals from those continents, either for trade or for philanthropic purposes. Primarily the religious interest underlies most of these establishments. Such is the case with the German 'Templar' colonies at Haifa, Jaffa, and Jerusalem, which have probably been the most successful of all. Living in sanitary houses and keeping regularly in touch with the Fatherland, they have resisted the enervating influence of the climate, and have set a healthy example of industry to the communities among which they are placed. The Jewish agricultural colonies are now planted in considerable numbers. Some of these appear to be successful enough, others however have a sadly forlorn aspect. Mention should also be made of the monastic communities, which carry on a variety of useful labours. They are hospices, where pilgrims and other travellers are received, and so they facilitate journeys through the country. They are in some cases, especially in Jerusalem, homes of learning, where important scientific research of various kinds is carried on. They are charitable institutions, and they carry on valuable educational work. The houses of those orders which devote themselves to manual labour offer useful object-lessons in scientific farming.

It seems to be the special privilege of the Anglo-Saxon race, on both sides of the Atlantic, to send out what may be described as 'freak' colonies—communities of worthy people who have upset their mental balance by irresponsible speculations about the Number of the Beast and kindred dangerous topics. Of such colonies there has been a long succession. But to compensate for these eccentrics, it should be said with all emphasis that the officers of the various legitimate mission agencies of both countries are doing a noble work, ministering to the spiritual and bodily needs of the dwellers in the land.

It will thus readily be imagined that the population, especially in the cities, is mixed to an extent beyond anything that European lands can shew.

This chapter is headed 'Till Yesterday' for it brings the history down to the end of a period already closed. In August 1908 the news burst on the people like a bomb-shell that the movement so long going on among the Armenians and among the exiled 'Young Turkish' party had been crowned with success, that the long-execrated absolute monarchy was over, and that a constitutional government had been inaugurated. The scenes that took place were probably unprecedented in the whole history of the land. The news had been sent to the Governor of Jerusalem (as to the governors of the other Turkish provinces) announcing the establishment of a constitution. That representative of the old _régime_ was startled, as well he might be : after consultation with his coadjutor, the Military Governor, they agreed to keep the news a secret, although the telegram contained express orders to publish it to the community without delay. A rumour leaked out, of course, that something had happened, and people began to come to the Governor's office to try to learn what it was. Not till the second day, however, did he consent to read

the telegram officially to the subordinates in his office:
and through them news reached the town at large.

The whole town as one man then assembled,
through the streets leading to the barracks, where
speeches were made by the leading officials. Badges,
with *Liberté, Egalité, Fraternité* printed upon them,
mysteriously made their appearance and were hawked
about for a halfpenny. And though the crowds were
so great and the pressure in the narrow streets so
close, not so much as a child was hurt on that happy
day. Next the whole mob, Muslims, Jews, and
Christians, went in a body to the Haram—the sacred
enclosure of the Holy Rock, the ancient Temple Site,
where without a permit and a military escort none
save the followers of Muhammad dare set their foot
—each singing the songs of their respective Faiths.
For once there was neither Jew nor Greek—all alike
were *Ottomans*! Supercilious old Muslim sheikhs
and bigoted Jewish rabbis might be seen embracing
in the streets. On all sides was heard the glad cry
hurriyeh—'liberty!'

A short six weeks later, people were beginning to
look each other in the face and to ask apprehensively
what was going to happen next. For the new-born
'liberty' was growing to a veritable Frankenstein's
monster, with many-sided and unexpected energies.
To give but one example: among other restrictions
that had been removed in the first outburst of

enthusiasm was a wholesome regulation against the importation and sale of firearms—and now every shop was selling thousands of the latest and best pattern of revolver to whoever chose to purchase. Shepherd boys of ten years of age might be seen strutting about with a couple of these murderous weapons in their belts. Even grown-up possessors of such dangerous toys could not resist the amusement of letting them off like popguns at all hours of the day and night. Till the novelty wore off—*experto crede*—it was difficult to sleep at night in Jerusalem merely on account of the noise of firearms going off at all hours ; and the danger of being hit by chance bullets was very considerable. All kinds of stories, some serious, some ridiculous, were being circulated, turning on the inconvenience arising from too suddenly granting liberty to a community not educated enough to distinguish that privilege from an illegitimate license. Throughout the country the sheikhs thought they saw their opportunity to regain the long suppressed power of their ancestors : and the consequent brawls filled the hospitals with wounded men. In the region of Samaria, for instance, the people of the village of Telluzeh raided the cattle of their neighbours in 'Asireh. A year before the people of the latter village would have gone to the Governor of Nablus, who would have quartered a soldier or two on the offenders—and these would have made the life of the Telluzeh people such a burden that sooner or later they would have restored the cattle or their value, if only to get rid of the incubus. Rough justice, perhaps, but fitted for a rough people. But now, instead, the 'Asireh people went to the descendant of their ancient tribal sheikh, who led them out to a regular pitched battle with the Telluzites, where two or three men were killed.

All over the country the same story was told—an alarming outbreak of lawlessness and crime of all kinds. It very soon became clear that the traditions of centuries of corruption and extortion on the one hand, of timidity or apathy on the other, and of selfishness on all sides, were not to be broken down because an old man was forced by circumstances to sign his imperial name on a sheet of paper.

There followed during the succeeding years, kaleidoscopic changes, all for the worse : and then came the world-shattering war. This has given a totally unexpected turn to the fortunes of Palestine : the end, as we write, is not yet in sight, and he would be a bold man who would venture to prophecy what a day may bring forth in the ancient land.

But over the land, day and night, floats down from the minarets the musical chant of the muezzin —*Allahu akbar !* *Allahu akbar !*

BIBLIOGRAPHY

Only a small selection can be mentioned from among the books on Palestine. RÖHRICHT, *Bibliotheca Geographica Palaestinae* (Berlin, 1890), enumerates 3515 books, issued between 333 A.D. and 1878 A.D. Many, very diverse in value, have been published since the latter date.

TRAVEL AND EXPLORATION

For early travellers see the *Palestine Pilgrims' Text Society's* translations (13 vols.) especially the *Wanderings* of FELIX FABRI (1480–3). BLISS, *The Development of Palestine Exploration* (London, 1906), gives a convenient summary. The most important later travellers are RAUWOLFF, *Beschreibung der Rais...inn die Morgenland* (1575): ZUALLART, *Il devotissimo viaggio di Gierusalemme* (1586): SANDYS, *Travailes containing...a Description of the Holy Land* (1610): QUARESMIO, *Elvcidatio Terrae Sanctae historica, theologica, moralis* (1616–26): MAUNDRELL, *A journey from Aleppo to Jerusalem* (1697): MORISON, *Relation historique d'un voyage nouvellement fait au Mont de Sinaï et à Jérusalem* (1697): POCOCKE, *Description of the East and some other Countries* (1743–5): VOLNEY, *Voyage en Syrie et en Egypte pendant les années 1783–5.*

RELAND, *Palaestina ex monumentis veteribus illustrata* (1714), is a compilation, still valuable, of facts known down to the date of publication. It is the point of departure for all the later scientific work. The chief explorers of the nineteenth century down to the establishment of the Palestine Exploration Fund were BURCKHARDT, SEETZEN, ROBINSON (1838–52), TOBLER (1845–65), LYNCH (1848), GUÉRIN (1852–75), DE SAULCY (1853), PIEROTTI (1863), whose names are sufficient to identify their contributions to research. Later come the explorers of the Palestine Exploration Fund, founded 1865: WILSON, WARREN, DRAKE, PALMER, CLERMONT-GANNEAU, KITCHENER, CONDER, PETRIE, BLISS. East of the Jordan SCHUMACHER, G. A. SMITH and MUSIL have worked. CONDER, *Tent Life in Palestine*, is a pleasantly written account of survey work in the country.

TOPOGRAPHY

In addition to the works of writers mentioned in the previous section see the *Map* of the Palestine Exploration Fund, and the companion descriptive volumes (*Survey of Western Palestine*, 7 vols., *Survey of Eastern Palestine*, 1 vol.). BAEDEKER'S *Guide* is thorough and accurate. RITTER, *Comparative Geography of Palestine and the Sinaitic Peninsula* (translation, Edinburgh, 1866), is very full up to the date of publication. No old books on Jerusalem are devoid of value, as they record features now much changed. For East of Jordan see in addition to writers mentioned above, BURTON and DRAKE, *Unexplored Syria*: MERRILL, *East of the Jordan*: CONDER, *Heth and Moab*: BRÜNNOW and VON DOMASZEWSKI, *Die Provincia Arabiens*: LIBBEY and HOSKINS, *The Jordan Valley and Petra*: DALMAN, *Petra*. Important maps, photographic and otherwise, have been made by the recent military expedition.

EXCAVATION

VINCENT, *Canaan d'après l'exploration récente* (1907), is the best summary. DRIVER, *Modern Research as illustrating the Bible* (1909), is the most convenient in English. The separate memoirs on the different excavations should be consulted for details. For the Galilean synagogues see MASTERMAN'S useful *Studies in Galilee* (1909).

ANTHROPOLOGY, FOLKLORE, &c.

There is no authoritative book, but much information can be gained from the volumes of the Quarterly Statement of the P. E. F., especially in papers by CLERMONT-GANNEAU and BALDENSPERGER. See also THOMSON, *The Land and the Book*: HANAUER, *Folklore of the Holy Land*: CURTISS, *Primitive Semitic Religion To-day*: W. R. SMITH, *Religion of the Semites* and *Kinship and Marriage in Early Arabia*: WELLHAUSEN, *Reste arabischen Heidenthums*: LAGRANGE, *Études sur les religions sémitiques*: BARTON, *A sketch of Semitic Origins*. S. A. COOK, *Religion of Ancient Palestine in the Second Millennium* B.C. (1908), is a convenient summary.

For the Bedawin, BURCKHARDT is still valuable: JAUSSEN, *Arabes au pays de Moab* (1908), is very important. For the fellahin, see WILSON, *Peasant Life in the Holy Land*.

For special points such as diseases, geology, climate, &c., any *modern* Encyclopaedia or Bible Dictionary may be consulted with advantage, the articles on such subjects being generally written by competent resident observers. See MASTERMAN, *Hygiene and Disease in Palestine in Modern and in Biblical Times*.

HISTORY

Prehistoric. BLANCKENHORN, *Ueber die Steinzeit und die Feuersteinartefakte in Syrien-Palästina* (Zeitschrift für Ethnologie, 1905, p. 447): ZUMOFFEN, *La Phénicie avant les Phéniciens* (privately printed, Beirut 1900): VINCENT, *Canaan*, concluding chapter. For the Beit Jibrin Caves, see BLISS, *Explorations in Palestine* (1900).

Old Testament History. PATON, *Early History of Syria and Palestine* (1902), is a convenient summary of modern critical views, and has a valuable bibliography. The various historical books of the O.T., interpreted by suitable commentaries, are the chief, often the only sources of information. W. MAX MÜLLER, *Asien und Europa*: the *Tell el-Amarna Letters* (ed. WINCKLER or KNUDTZON). and MASPERO's three large volumes of history, supply the necessary setting for the specific history of Palestine itself. For Crete consult BURROWS, *The Discoveries in Crete*: LAGRANGE, *La Crète ancienne*. For the Philistines see NOORDTZIJ, *De Filistijnen* (Kampen, 1905): MACALISTER, *The Philistines* (Schweich Lectures): G. A. SMITH, *Historical Geography of the Holy Land* and *Jerusalem, the Topography, Economics, and History from the earliest Times to A.D. 70* are indispensable.

Later Periods. Consult SACHAU, *Drei aramäische Papyrusurkunden aus Elephantine*: SCHÜRER, *Jewish People in the Time of Christ*: MORRISON, *Jews under Roman Rule*: MARGOLIOUTH, *Mohammed*: LE STRANGE, *Palestine under the Moslems*: MICHAUD, *History of the Crusades*: BESANT and PALMER, *Jerusalem, the City of Herod and Saladin*: CONDER, *Latin Kingdom of Jerusalem*. For architectural remains of these periods see the works of DE VOGÜÉ: REY, *Monuments de l'architecture militaire des Croisés*: *report* of the Princeton University archaeological expedition, 1902–5: the Byzantine Research Fund's recently published *monograph* on the Church of the Nativity at Bethlehem.

JOURNALS

Quarterly Statement, Palestine Exploration Fund: *Zeitschrift des deutschen Palästinavereins*: *Mittheilungen der deutschen Orientgesellschaft*: *Revue biblique*: *Recueil d'archéologie orientale*: and many others, too numerous to specify, devoted to theology, Biblical criticism, and archaeological research.

INDEX

'Abbasides **111**
'Abd el-Melek 109
Absalom 57; tomb of 75
Abu Dis 17
Acheulean flints 9
Acre 117, 120
Aegean civilization 31
Aelia Capitolina 101
Agriculture 1, 7, 122
Ahab 68, 87
Ahmed the Butcher 119
Ahmose drives out Hyksos 46
'Akili Agha 119
Alashia 43
Alexander the Great 74
Alphabet 59, 61 changes in Hebrew 76
Amalekites 20
Amen-Hotep III 47
'Amman 9, 122
Amos 63, 69, 89
Amulets 13, 33, 37, 44
Anakim 22
Antelias 10
Anthropomorphism 92
Antigonus 74
Antiochus Epiphanes 74, 76
Apollophanes, tomb of 77
Arab art 109
Arab immigration 29, 108
Arabia 26, 27, 107
Aramaic language 77
Architecture, Greek 75; Arab 111
Aristobulus **95**
Arnon 7
Art, Arab **109**

Asa 88
Ashdod 22, 24
Assyrians 28, 38, 61, 70, 71, 119
Augustus 101
Azariah son of Oded 88

Babylonians 28, 61, 71
Baitogabra 25
Bedawin 20, 45, 47, 72, 79, 80
Beersheba 2, 122
Beia son of Gulati 47
Beirut 5
Beitin, *see* Bethel
Beit Jala 107
Beit Jibrin 17, 24, 25, 77
Belfort, castle of 7
Ben-Hadad 67, 68
Bethel 18, 67
Bethlehem 104, 107, 116
Beth-Shan 54
Blanckenhorn 11
Bordeaux Pilgrim 105
Burial, neolithic 15; Semitic 31, 42
el-Buttauf 6
Byzantine Churches 106
Byzantium 32, 38

Cairns 18
Calves 86
Canaanites 53
Capernaum 100
Captain of Host of the Lord 86
Captivities 70
Carmathians 111
Carmel **4**

Carpenters 44

Caves 41; dwellings 12, 23, 24; sacred 80; scribings 11

Character of modern inhabitants 123

Chellean flints 9

Chemosh 87

Chinnereth 3

Chorazin 104

Chosroes 106

Churches 106: see Holy Sepulchre

Circle, stone, at Bethel 18

Cities in Palestine 33; abandonment of 97

City life described 36, 37

Clermont-Ganneau 18, 20, 86

Climate of Palestine 7

Cnossos 49

Colonists, Jewish 125; European and American 32, 124

Cosmogony 92

Cow figures 90

Cremation 15

Crete 31, 49, 65; scripts of 62

Crusades 32, 38, 112

Curse on Palestine, alleged 29

Cyprus 43

Cyrus 73

Damascus 121

Date of earliest occupations 11

David 56, 64, 86, 87

Dead Sea 3, 9

Deborah 86

Déchelette 9

Deities of Semites 39

Demons 82

ed-Der'a 25

Desert, Arabian 2

Development of Palestine 121

Diseases of Palestine 8

Dolmens 17

Dor 53

Dome of the Rock 109, 121

Drunkenness 67

Egypt and Egyptians 31, 39, 45, 61; their relations with Palestine 33; Jewish settlements in 72; Palestine under domination of 118

Eli 68

Elijah 68, 85, 88

Emim 20

Ephraim 29, 52; mountains of 2

Esdraelon, see Jezreel

Ethan, Heman, Calcol, and Darda 64

European colonists, see Colonists

Evil Eye 37

Excavation, results of 31

Exodus 27

Ezekiel 71

Ezion-Geber 67

Ezra 73

Fakhr ed-Din 119

False weights 37, 44

Fenish 22, 58

First Semitic Immigration 29

Flavia Neapolis 102

Flint 8, 13, 43

Foreign influences 31, 42, 69; place-names 102

Galilee, dolmens in 17; mountains of 6; sea, 3

Gates, city 36

Gath 22, 24

Gaza 22, 24

Gezer 10–12, 17, 25, 33, 42, 47, 58, 65, 71, 90, 91

Giants 21

Gideon 86

Gilboa 53, 56
Godfrey of Boulogne 113
Goldsmiths 44
Gordon's Tomb 105
Graffiti 13–15
Greeks 22, 38; culture of 73, 74; influence of 32, 76; language 77, 102

Habiru 29
Hadad the Edomite 67
Hadrian 101
Hakim, Caliph 111
Hannah 68
Harajel 11
Hattin 115
Hauran 7; dolmens in 17
Hebron 2, 22, 24
Helena, Empress 104
Hermon, Mount 2
Herod 74, 95; his buildings 96, 97
High Places 40, 42, 84, 88
Hiram 65
Hittites 22, 50
Hivites 20
Hizmeh 18
Holy Sepulchre 104, 112
Horites 20
Houses 30, 34, 37
Huleh, lake 3
Hyrcanus 95

Ibrahim Pasha 120
Identification of sites 100
Ikhnaton 47
Influence of neighbouring civilizations 83
Iron, introduction of 43, 59
Israelite immigration 52

Jabesh-Gilead 85

Jaffa 1, 4, 6, 120
Jaulan, dolmens in 17
Jebusites 20
Jehoshaphat 67, 69
Jephthah 86
Jerash 122
Jeremiah 72
Jeroboam I 86; II 69
Jerusalem 2, 6, 48, 52, 56, 101, 121, 126; restoration of 73; siege of 96
Jews 73; settle in Tiberias 102
Jezebel 68, 69
Jezreel 5, 6, 53
Jifna 107
Jordan, 2, 9
Joshua 22, 86
Judaea, mountains of 5, 6, 8
Judah 29, 52
Judges, Book of 59, 86
Jupiter, temple of 101

Kabur Beni Isra'in 18
Kais 29, 119, 120
Kenites 52
Khan Minyeh 100
Kharezmians 118

Lagash 32
Language of Philistines 57
Law, Book of 74
Lebban 6
Litany Valley 7
Literature, Hebrew, development of 64
Lugalzaggizi 32

Maccabees 38, 74
Magdalenian Age 10, 11
Malaria 8, 115
Mareshah, Marissa 25
Maritime Plain 4

Masonry 66
Megalithic monuments 17, 18
Megiddo 65
Menhirs 18
Mer'ash, see Mareshah
Merj el-Ghuruk 6
Merom, Waters of 3
Mesopotamia 27
Metal, use of 13, 26, 29, 30, 43, 59
Micah 86
Midianites 20, 53
Milcom 87
Milk and honey 29
Millstones 13
Missionaries 125
Moab, Moabites 2, 53; dolmens
    in 17, 18; flints in 8; moun-
    tains of 6
Mode of life, Palaeolithic 8
Mojib 7
Monarchy, Hebrew 63
Monasteries 125
Monotheism 38
Mongols 118
Moses 85
Mother-goddess, Semitic 39
Mountain system 5
Mousterian scrapers 10
Muhammad 27, 68, 82, 107
Muhammad Ali 120
Muhammadan conquest of Pales-
    tine 108
Muhammadanism 32, 38

Naaman 87
Nabal 67
Nabataeans 27
Nablus 71, 102
Naboth 68
Napoleon I 120
Natives of Palestine, character-
    istics of 34, 123

Naval energies of Solomon 66
Nehemiah 57, 73
Neolithic culture 12
Nephilim 21, 22
Notre-Dame de France, museum
    of 9

Olives, Mount of 104
Olive-yards and olive presses 45
'Omar 108
Omayyades 111; mosque of 121
Omri 69
'Oreimeh 100

Palaeolithic man in Palestine 8
Palestine, description of 1
Patagonians 21
Pax Romana, influence of 97
People of Arabia, movements of
    27
People of the Sea 50
Perizzites 20
Persian Period 73
Peter the Hermit 112
Petra 9
Philistines 22, 38, 53, 56, 72;
    culture of 57; settlement of,
    in Palestine 50
Phoenicia, Phoenicians 8, 10, 61,
    65, 66
Pig, beliefs concerning 16
Pilgrim road 2
Pilgrims 104
Pillars 30
Place-names, foreign 102
Plaques with goddess figure 90, 91
Pompey 74, 95
Potters, pottery 13, 44, 66
Potters' stamps 76
Potter's Wheel 13, 30, 42
Pre-Semitic races 15, 20, 21
Prophet of Bethel 67

Prophets 89
Ptolemy Soter **74**
Public works, recent **122**
Purasati 50

Quarrels 37
Queen of Heaven 90

Rachel, tomb of 20
Ramessu III 50
Red Sea fleet 66, 67
Religion, iron avoided in 60;
   Neolithic 16; Palestinian 38;
   Semitic 30
Renan 69
Rephaim 20, **22**, 25, 26, 30
"Return of the Jews" 93
Revolution, effects of Turkish 126
Rhinoceros, woolly 11
Rhodian wine 75
Roman engineering works 40;
   remains in Palestine 102
Rome 32
Rum 22 : *see* Greeks

Sacrifice, place of 16
Salah ed-Din 115, 118
Samaria 8, 68, 96, 97, 101
Samaritans 71, 72
Samson 54
Samuel 55, 86; Book of 59
Sarcophagus of Alexander 75
Saul 55, 56
Scarabs 33
Schumacher 17
Scribings, Cave 11 : *see* also
   Graffiti
Scriptural passages quoted :
   Genesis vi. 1, 21, **79**; xxiii.
     22
   Exodus xx. 25, 61
   Numbers v. 11, 79

Scriptural passages (*cont.*):
   Joshua v. 13, 86; xi. 21, 22
   Judges vi. 2, 24
   1 Samuel i. 14, 68 ; xiii. 9-22,
     60
   1 Kings iv. 31-33, 64; vi. 7, 61;
     ix. 27, 67; xi. 14, 67; xiii.
     11, 67, xv. 20, 3
   Nehemiah xiii. 24, 57
   Isaiah lvii. 5-6, 42
   Jeremiah vii. 18, 90; xliv. 13,
     18, 90
   Acts viii. 5, 101
   Revelation xvi. 16, 5
Scripts, *see* Crete, Alphabet
Seasons 7
Sebaste 101 : *see* Samaria
Selman, Sheikh 40
Semites, characteristics of 67 ;
   immigrations 27; languages 28;
   origin 26; types 28
Sharon, plain of 1
Shechem 102
Sheikh domination 118, 119
Sheikhs' tombs 33, 39
Shepherd kings 45
Shiloh 55
Sidon 75
Siloam pool and tunnel 70
Simeonites 52
Simon Bar-Cochba 101
Sirocco 8
Sollas 9
Solomon 63, 64, 87
Solomon's Pools 97
Solutré 10
Spies, the 20
Spindle-whorls 15
Springs 40, 80
Statuettes of terracotta **75**
Stones, standing 18
Surṭabeh 86

Sutu 29
Synagogues of Galilee 103

Taanach 65
Talhum 100
Talmud, Jerusalem 102
Tekoa 99
Tell es-Safi 97
Temple, Egyptian, in Palestine 39; of Solomon 65
Templar colonies 124
Teraphim 86
Textiles 10, 15
Thutmose III, conquests of 46
Tiberias 102
Titus 74, 96
Tigranes 95
Trades in Palestine 42–46
Trees, sacred 80
Tribal god, development of 81
Tripoli 5
Tunnel for water 40, 41
Turks 118

Unoriginality of Palestinian civilization 32
Uzziah 69

Vespasian 102
Vincent 18
Virgin's Fountain 70

Walls, city 36
Weavers 44
Wells 40
Wheel, Potter's, see Potters

Yaman 27, 29, 119, 120
Yapakhi 47

Zamzummim 20, 25
Zerubbabel 73
Zimri 67
Zumoffen 10
Zuzim 20, 25